My Farewell to the Yellow House

István Hollós

Translated by
Adrian Courage

1968

First published in English 2024 by 1968 Press

'Búcsúm a Sárga Háztól' by István Hollós was first published in Hungarian by Genius Kiadás, Budapest, 1927

The translation of this book was supported by a UKRI Frontier Research Grant [grant number EP/X022064/1]

ISBN: 9781919601953 (pbk & ebk)

Printed and bound in Great Britain by Clays Ltd, Elcograf S.p.A.

1968 Press, London

important little books in psychoanalysis

Important Little Books in Psychoanalysis

Series edited by
Raluca Soreanu, Lizaveta van Munsteren
and the FREEPSY collective

Contents

Translator's Note

It was a strange twist of fate that I was commissioned to translate this book. I am half Hungarian and half English, and have worked as a translator since 2000, but that is only part of the story. Three years before this book came to me, and just a few kilometres from Hollós' Yellow House on another Buda hill, I had my own 'procession to Calvary' on a freezing cold January morning. Gripped by psychosis, I ran through the streets naked. After several weeks in hospital and two years of suffering from the side effects of various medications, my bipolar disorder stabilised and I was left pondering the nature of my condition. It was then that this book landed in my lap. Aside from the professional challenge, it appears to have answered a lot of the questions about mental illness that were burning in my soul.

The main theme of the book is the relationship between the 'lunatics' in the 'madhouse' and the people of sound mind in the outside world. Today, as then, we continue to use the same or similar words as insults in everyday life—most likely in every language on Earth. Few people consider that 'mania' might be a medical condition, or that casually calling someone 'crazy', 'insane', 'mad', or a 'lunatic' is no different to making an unfounded suggestion that they have a debilitating physical illness.

Briefly flicking through the book during a consultation, my Hungarian psychiatrist (who, as a 'man of medicine', had never heard of the work) immediately picked out two words, 'elmebeteg' and 'tébolyda'. He said these are words he can no longer use in his profession. Yet you hear them every day, I thought to add. The former, meaning 'person who is sick of mind', where 'mind' should be understood to be something closer to 'psyche' than to 'brain', is still in common use today. It is unfortunate that we do not have such a word in English that takes sickness of the mind seriously yet can be used in the vernacular—and generally does so with more than a hint of pity, much like that we would afford someone with any other health condition. Without such a word, or indeed the word 'beteg', which means both 'patient' and 'sufferer', it is difficult to get across the key idea that Hollós is trying to convey, namely that perceptions of mental illness are very different from without to from within. That those with mental illness are both seriously 'crazy' and seriously 'ill'—and that it is all a matter of perception.

At the other end of the spectrum, 'tébolyda' is an archaic word I have alternately translated as 'asylum' or 'madhouse'—although 'bedlam' may be the closest alternative. The two words I chose are intended to reflect that the official name of the Yellow House was initially the 'Királyi Tébolyda'—'Royal Bedlam'. 'Tébolyda' is today an almost endearingly derogatory term, just as 'bedlam' is now no longer used so often as a nickname for the Bethlem Royal Hospital in London, or any other psychiatric institution for that matter, but to refer to the state of madness you would expect to find in such a place. That is the nature of words associated with mental illness, after a while, their meaning becomes warped, making it necessary for more 'scientific' and sterile terms to take their place. Take the example of 'shell shock', now known as Post-Traumatic Stress Disorder, or PTSD for short. It could be said that this supports Hollós' assertion that there exists a wall constructed to guard the insane from the sane, physically, psychologically, and linguistically.

The task of the translator of historical documents is always to find a balance between how language was used at the time of writing and what is acceptable today. In the case of this book, Hollós was very much poking fun at the establishment of the day and his own use of language reflects this. It is highly ironic that this 'bedlam' is such a grandiose palace of a building dropped into a leafy hillside in Budapest. That this institution should be known to Hungarian readers is taken for granted by Hollós but will not be familiar to the international audience. This was difficult to convey in the translation but should be noted in considering that the Yellow House was highly influential in its time, and that Hollós' writing would have carried significant weight, even with its intentionally irreverent style.

It is interesting, for instance, that 'lunatic asylum' has its own Wikipedia entry chronicling the history of institutions around the world that were once just like our Yellow House. Yet, as Hollós repeatedly points out, the term immediately conjures up fearful visions of wild-eyed crazies (not infrequently referred to as 'inmates') rattling barred windows. Inhumane treatment of the mentally ill no doubt, but how much have things really changed in practice despite the creeping changes in what language is deemed appropriate? Our terminology may have evolved, but has our understanding of mental illness really moved on? It is amazing reading this work that, despite the debatable linguistic issues, the message remains as revolutionary and relevant as ever. All this with scarcely any mention of particular diagnostic categories. Which, Hollós would argue, is how it should be. The mentally ill are people, too, no matter what we call them. It is with this in mind that I found it appropriate to use the terminology and expressions of the time as far as possible.

Hollós adopts an at-times ironic tone, one that in turns mocks society's commonplaces of thought about the patient, the doctor, and their relationship. He intentionally uses words inappropriately and provocatively to the point where the reader cannot be sure he is to be taken seriously. I have tried to convey the typically Hungarian, and some would say Jewish, ambiguity of Hollós' writing in my translation.

Hollós, too, relies heavily on analogy and poetry, just as he reveres poets for their roles in exposing the ills of society. It is perhaps no coincidence that Hollós ended up in the Yellow House later in life, perhaps as a poet himself. And so in his writing style Hollós attempts to bridge the chasm between doctor and patient with a consistency I only came to appreciate on the second or third reading. As a translator, it was a genuine pleasure to hear the author's 'voice' grow more powerful as my familiarity with the book increased. This was a rare joy that perhaps only those of us who must immerse ourselves in a piece of writing in this way can truly understand. As a keen admirer, I have tried to capture Hollós' frequently profane worldview in the English version.

Despite being in the thick of it, Hollós distances himself from a profession, and society, he considers corrupt. Linguistically, he adopts a tone of outrage, while also addressing the complex issues associated with the burgeoning discipline of psychoanalysis as championed by Sigmund Freud and his Hungarian compatriot Sándor Ferenczi. He does so by using thick, poetic analogies, and at times the odd line of poetry that is a long way from what we now associate with psychiatry. I hope I have managed to reflect this in the English while conveying the important messages about the effects of unconscious drives on the individual and the masses that are still so relevant today—and all too often forgotten, in my opinion. These echoes of the psychoanalytic movement make a crucial connection between Freud's theory and the practicalities and inescapable difficulties of treating mental illness. The knowledge of the early psychoanalytical movement in Vienna and Budapest I have picked up through my research and other translation work was critical in this regard.

Finally, Hollós must also be praised for his disarmingly succinct writing style that makes this book such a refreshingly easy read. This made my job as translator all the easier and more enjoyable.

Adrian Courage, 2024

Editors' Introduction

My Farewell to the Yellow House is a manifesto that aims to rethink the practical and theoretical bases of psychiatric care. To follow István Hollós' own words, it aims to break down the walls of the asylum. From the outset, we can read 'asylum' not strictly as an institution, a place, or a building, but as a psychic state, one where the demarcations between the 'sane' and the 'insane' are strong and unquestionable. The book also offers a sharp critique of society's gaze upon madness. Although it was written nearly a century ago, it pulsates with contemporary questions. It approaches the *fear of madness* as a socially and psychically produced phenomenon, leading to exclusion, splitting, and various forms of authoritarianism. Through this unusual book, István Hollós joins a long line of radical psychiatrists, who were keenly aware of the societal importance of studying the 'politics of madness'[1]: François Tosquelles, Ronald Laing, Franco Basaglia, Franca Ongaro, Franz Fanon, Félix Guattari, and Jean Oury, to name but a few. What brings together these otherwise very different thinkers is an emancipatory agenda in relation to psychiatric care, often drawing on various kinds of knowledge, from psychoanalysis, and psychiatry, to neurology, phenomenology, anthropology, philosophy, aesthetics, and social theory. To be alert to the politics of madness means to be able to ask unusual questions such as, in Hollós' words: 'How did the mentally ill influence wars and revolutions?' (p.111). It also means turning on its head the question of who needs to be healed and who is doing the healing. As radical psychiatrists have argued, it is the psychiatric hospital, or the asylum, or even the doctor-patient relationship that needs to be cured. Tuning to the voice of the patients, Hollós writes: 'We are the sick, but it is you healthy people who must be healed! Through us, the dreaming heroes, storytellers and lunatics, the axis of history creaks towards new, incredible cities and possibilities for life' (p.121).

With Hollós, the reader will experience in the pages of this book a series of shifts in perspective, reorientations, and even some temporary disorientations. All these are part of a politics of representation of madness, which necessarily involves forms of understanding that take *the other* seriously. The book you are holding in your hands is not one of psychiatric diagnosis, neither one of psychoanalytic theory, but one that weaves its own forms of insight, guided by psychoanalytic principles; and also guided by an orientation to the other and their enigmas, and by a capacity to be affected by the other, which amounts to 'social love'. As Hollós tells us:

> As much as it pains me, my friend, I must also speak of things that are labelled scientific; but I do not do so in the interests of science. I have only one goal: to liberate the mentally ill. And for this, it is necessary to understand them. You must become conscious of the fact that the healthy and the mentally ill do not stand face to face like man and monster. This must be understood! And so the liberation of the mental patient is not a matter of humanism, but one of understanding (p.86).

My Farewell to the Yellow House is thus a unique writing, one that takes the risk of unfolding in between genres. It is neither memoir nor biography, although the vignettes that Hollós constructs for the reader are informed by actual episodes, encounters, and scenes of the asylum. In a memorable passage of the book (see 'Truth and Comedy'), the reader will come across the description of a visit to the asylum by a company of actors who were interested in how to accurately portray madness in their theatrical performances. The actors appear rather disappointed by the fact that the patients do not present as 'mad enough' for their expectations. When the time of the public performance comes, they offer their audiences a caricatural and hyperbolic portrayal of the lunatics, which by confirming commonly held views, is met with great enthusiasm by the public. We know from archival sources[2] and a published diary[3] that asylum visits by companies of actors actually took place, and so the scene that Hollós assembles for us is rooted in day-to-day experience in the institution. Despite not being a theoretical book in psychoanalysis, *My Farewell to the Yellow House* is quietly organised around psychoanalytic constructs, such as regression, and the life and death drives, in dialogue with Sigmund Freud; or betrayal, in resonance with Sándor Ferenczi and his idea of the confusion of tongues between adults and the child, fully articulated only later in 1933.[4] Despite not being a book of clinical cases, the author talks in vivid ways about patients and doctors, and what is passed between them. In Hollós' book, the doctor makes mistakes, and is able to reflect on their own role and power position. Ultimately, Hollós resonates with many voices in radical psychiatry by treating the asylum as a symptom of societal repression and denial. As he writes: 'Each prohibition is a little yellow house unto itself. Then, all of a sudden, there are a great number of little yellow houses, and all those locked-in desires break out. That's why people built the big Yellow House. The Yellow House is itself a symptom in which the repressed, the forbidden returns' (p.144).

The book opens with the voice of a fictional character, Doctor Telemach Pfeiflein,[5] who entrusts István Hollós the manuscript on the Yellow House for publication. The first name of the fictional character, Telemach, is a reference to the son of Odysseus in Greek mythology. For the educated reader of the age, the name might have also evoked the popular eighteenth-century novel *The Adventures of Telemachus,* written by Bishop François Fénelon, tutor of Louis XIV's grandson. This novel is a didactic work, a 'mirror for princes' describing the principles of wise governing through exciting adventures. The hero of Fénelon's book is Mentor, the tutor of Telemachus: the whole narrative is built around his expositions on the art of governing. Mentor is against war, luxury, and selfishness, while he proclaims the importance of brotherhood and the necessity of altruism. By choosing Telemachus as an alter ego, Hollós puts himself in the role of a disciple always seeking new insights. Hollós had significant experience with 'difficult cases' and he was able to reflect on his own development as a psychiatrist, and on the pitfalls of the psychiatric method of the time.

The small volume you are holding in your hands is also the fruit of immense struggle. It is a text that carries the weight of the twentieth century, with its wars, persecutions, deaths, dislocations, authoritarianisms, and forms of silencing. As a psychiatrist, Hollós struggled against the dogmatic outlook of his times, and relied on psychoanalysis to arrive at new and less hierarchical questions about madness. In the third part of *My Farewell to the Yellow House,* Hollós is in dialogue with Sigmund Freud, showing his readers the importance of the death drive in psychic life. As a person of Jewish origin, Hollós knew many forms of persecution. In 1922, he lost his lead psychiatrist post, as a result of the *numerus clausus* laws. In a letter written to Paul Federn on 17 February 1946,[6] Hollós recounts a chilling episode in which he and his wife were taken barefoot to the Danube, to be executed, as part of a group of around 200 Jewish people, only escaping through an unlikely intervention. In 1952, Hollós develops ideas of persecution and suffers a psychotic breakdown. He is treated in the Mental Care Department of the Public Hospital of the 13th District from 1952 until his death in 1957. In 1955, he resides in a private room of the Lipótmező, The Yellow House, as a respected visitor and a receiver of care.

To walk alongside Hollós and into the space of this book, it is important to discern some of the shapes of both psychoanalytic and psychiatric networks in Budapest in the 1920s and 1930s—two facets of Hollós' thinking and practice. In these decades, psychoanalysis in Budapest was marked by an unusual pluridisciplinarity, based on intense exchanges of several avant-garde intellectuals, including writers, musicians, painters, psychoanalysts, medical doctors, anthropologists, lawyers, economists, and psychiatrists. Already in 1908, Sándor Ferenczi met Sigmund Freud, an encounter which was to mark the history of psychoanalysis. The same year, the fortnightly journal *Nyugat (The West, 1908-1941)* was launched, a publication which was transformative for Hungarian cultural life, and which offered a forum for both literature and science. Psychoanalysis had its place in its pages too. Forums of similar importance were the medical weekly *Gyógyászat* (*Therapeutics*, 1861-1944), and the sociology journal *Huszadik Század* (*The Twentieth Century*, 1900-1919). Hollós had a close relationship with the founders of *Nyugat* and with several noted contributors, including Ignotus (Hugó Veigelsberg), Frigyes Karinthy, Dezső Kosztolányi, Milán Füst, Sándor Ferenczi, and Róbert Berény—the latter belonging to *The Eight*, the avant-garde group of painters who brought innovations to pictorial art in Hungary. To borrow an image from Pál Ignotus (the son of the *Nyugat* founder mentioned above), this milieu was 'a Bloomsbury on the Danube', progressive and opposed to any restrictions to artistic creativity. As Pál Ignotus stresses, the imagination of the radical intellectuals of Budapest was linked to

Latin elegance through nostalgia and to German culture through geographical links, while it also eagerly seized on all experiments in style and thought. Recalling scenes of his youth, Pál Ignotus comments on the leading role of literature in Hungarian culture as follows: 'So great was the power of literature over science, and of rhetoric over literature, in a Hungary forever linked to the memory of 1848, that without its trumpet-like conclusions even statistical analyses would have seemed shocking and meaningless to readers.' [7]

Hollós was part of this plurisidisciplinary conversation. Just like Ferenczi, he published in *Nyugat* articles that offered a psychoanalytic interpretation of cultural phenomena. In his article 'Egy versmondó betegről' ['On a Patient Who Recites Poems'] of 1914, he wrote about the sources of poetic inspiration. In 'Nemzeti Géniusz és pszichoanalízis' ['National Genius and Psychoanalysis'] of 1929, he analysed Hungarian words and expressions related to dreams and sleep so as to demonstrate for Hungarian detractors of psychoanalysis that the Hungarian 'popular mind' seems to prove Freud's dream theory in its idiomatic creations. Ultimately, Hollós joins a number of thinkers who were not interested in being anchored by a single discourse, and were passionate about crossing disciplinary borders, about spaces between the public and the private, and about inter-forms and inter-genres of writing.[8] In Hollós' *My Farewell to the Yellow House*, references to psychoanalysts Sigmund Freud and Sándor Ferenczi are present alongside those to the famous poets Dániel Berzsenyi (1776–1836) and Sándor Petőfi (1823–1849).

Hollós had an equally important connection with the psychiatric milieu. We can imagine the psychiatric model in Budapest in his time as a Janus-faced one. The two faces of the coin meant that on the one hand psychiatry in Budapest was somewhat 'delayed' in terms of the European standards of institutionalisation, and on the other hand it was progressive in showing a preference for no-restraint methods in the asylums.[9] Gusztáv Oláh (1857-1944), a French-oriented, Pinel-respecting psychiatrist, and director of the Yellow House, advocated for taking psychiatric treatments beyond the walls of the big public asylums and hospital wards and into the community. Alienists such as Károly Bolyó, Jakab Salgó, Jenő Konrád, Károly Lechner, or Kálmán Páldy resonated with Oláh's approach. László Epstein, a well-known alienist who played an active part in the association of psychiatrists and alienists, claimed as early as 1907: 'Since we do not have raging wards, we also do not have raging patients'.[10] However, he also admitted that patient management was hardly possible without resorting to some sort of restraint or occasional use of the strait-jacket.

The no-restraint tradition in the Hungarian model emerged partly from the practices of the respected private asylum, the Schwartzer Private Institute, operating in Buda in the 1850s, which was considered 'the cradle of the mental pathological studies in Hungary'.[11] This private enterprise created the 'family world' of the asylum, mirroring the system of the bourgeois family, ruled by the charismatic and authoritative head of the household who protects and disciplines.[12] At the biggest state public asylum, Lipótmező (Leopoldfeld, the Yellow House where Hollós spent most of his career), opened in 1868, the asylum alienist had decisive powers regarding admission, discharging and guardianship, or '"custody and care" of incurable and dangerous patients from all over the Kingdom'.[13]

For instance, according to Gusztáv Oláh's memoir, Gyula Niedermann, the charismatic doctor-director of Lipótmező between 1884 and 1899, was a caring and beloved despot: *der Pascha von Leopoldfeld*. These strong and revered asylum directors often confronted the psychiatrists working at the university clinic in Budapest. Here, the primary tasks were research and the education of medical students, while treatment was relegated to a secondary place. It was mostly the asylum alienists, the *pater familias* of the psychiatric institutions, who initiated reforms at the crowded state asylums. One of their most effective initiatives was the institution of family care, a system of treatment, mostly based on the model of the Belgian Gheel Colony and adjusted to the local features of the Hungarian psychiatric environment. Among its advocates we can see major mental doctors, e.g., Kálmán Pándy, Rudolf Fabinyi, István Zsakó, and István Hollós himself.

The institution of family care, launched in 1905 in Dicsőszentmárton/Târnăveni (situated in Transylvania, next to Nagyszeben/Sibiu), was centred on placing incurable patients in village households, or newly built colonies close to asylums, or bigger hospital wards, where the host families received income in return. The institution of family care proved to be an ingenious solution. Patients deemed incurable were revived in the fresh air of the countryside, surrounded by members of the community. The state paid lesser costs compared to asylum care. Often, the living conditions of the host families improved as well, in an attempt to comply with the regulations stipulated for 'receiving' the patients.[14]

In this landscape, István Hollós gained the reputation of an extraordinarily dedicated, patient-centred, and empathic psychiatrist. In 1922, in an exceptional letter held by the Ferenczi House Archive in Budapest, psychiatrist and asylum director Gusztáv Oláh has the task, within the predicament of the *numerus clausus* laws, to dismiss Hollós as chief physician. It is thus important to note that Hollós knew a forced farewell to the Yellow House, linked to political circumstances and the rise of fascism. The letter vibrates with tones of deep professional recognition, collegiality, and tragic regret for this destitution. As Oláh writes: 'You as chief doctor managed the sensitive and demanding asylum ward not only with dedication, but with a style of artistic excellence, which, in addition to Your superior qualities as a psychiatrist, can only be made possible by Your love for the patients.'[15] The professional relationship between Oláh and Hollós was a long-standing one: as a young doctor Hollós had impressed the senior alienist Oláh, during a short internship in the Angyalföld Asylum in the summer of 1898.[16]

Hollós' 'mark' as a psychiatrist was his extensive application of psychoanalysis to psychiatric treatment. He set the scene for the introduction of the 'open door system' in Hungary, which gave patients greater freedom and a better chance for recovery.[17] From 1908 onwards, Hollós focuses in his writing on assessing the conditions of mental hospitals and on the need for talking therapy, while also being aware of the obstacles to it. Analysing patient turnover at Lipótmező over a period of forty years, Hollós complained that a patient who did not speak Hungarian (because he/she had been transferred from a non-Hungarian speaking locality of multi-ethnic Hungary) had no access to the most elementary instrument of psychotherapy: the language his/her psychotherapist spoke.[18] In the same article Hollós came to the conclusion that the biggest single obstacle to treatment and recovery was the very conditions in mental hospitals at the time. Hollós was also a supporter of the institution of family care, and he maintained this support even during the post-war years. At that time, partly because of the forced industrialization of the 1950s in the communist Hungary, the family care treatment was obliterated.

In the pages of *My Farewell to the Yellow House*, Hollós abdicates the role of *pater familias*. The psychiatrist of this book does not occupy a place of care and control, but one of questioning, which includes self-questioning. The imaginary of the book is an anti-patriarchal and anti-authoritarian one, where all-knowing fathers and the matrix of the traditional family dissolve and crumble. Indeed, we seem to exit the world of the traditional family, and take steps toward the 'chosen' family, either within the walls of the asylum, or outside it. It is a world of kinship. Rather than a biologically bound 'set' that is forced to live with madness, we meet a different 'set' bound together by a kind of acceptance of sharing the experience of mental breakdown and repair. This is perhaps what Hollós means by his enigmatic term 'social love'. In a world scarce of fathers, we meet more figures of mothers, sisters, and children; but also, importantly, diffuse figures that are not cast in familial roles. The perspectives shift, the inside becomes the outside, and invites new thoughts on society's gaze on madness. The doctor listens closely to the patients and tunes into their voices.

•

In *My Farewell to the Yellow House* Hollós' voice is poetic and refuses to resort to the psychoanalytic or psychiatric registers. However, Hollós' psychoanalytic-psychiatric work had another side, anchored in the professional discourse of his time: between 1922 and 1933, he published a series of in-depth scientific papers. During this period, he was also close to Ferenczi. The *Yellow House*, therefore, offers a different entry into the issues that preoccupied him. Hollós' studies at this time were published predominantly in German. Several of them appeared in the top psychoanalytic journals of the time: *Internationale Zeitschrift für Psychoanalyse* and *Imago*. Curiously, these studies did not appear in Hungarian even when they were written versions of Hollós' Hungarian lectures in Budapest. (By contrast, *My Farewell to the Yellow House* was published first in Hungarian in 1927, and only the year after in German.) In 1933, Hollós published the significant study titled 'The Work of the Dream and Mental Illnesses', in a volume commemorating Ferenczi's death. After 1933, Hollós published very little, either in German or Hungarian, which may be related to the grief Hollós had felt at the loss of Ferenczi.

His studies published in German around the time of the *Yellow House* were very significant. Some were comprehensive metapsychological studies.[19] Others were explorations of the presence of psychoanalytic ideas in the history of psychiatry.[20] Others were psychiatric case discussions, but unlike the *Yellow House*, they were embedded in the psychoanalytic and psychiatric scientific discourses. One of these, 'On the Sense of Time' (1922), interprets the temporal delusions of psychotic patients related to their age and birth time, to arrive at a metapsychological formulation on the relationship between psychic and bodily visions of time and rhythmicity. In 1923, Hollós gave a lecture on 'The Psychoneurosis of a Premature Infant' at a meeting of the Hungarian Psychoanalytical Association, just before the publication of Otto Rank's *The Trauma of Birth*. The subject was the psychoanalytic interpretation of childbirth, and close to Rank's concept of it.[21]

In addition to the case histories and writings on the history of psychoanalytic therapy, Hollós also published substantial metapsychological summaries. In one of these papers, he examined the reality of the patient's self-interpretation, pointing to how 'a peculiar communication between the conscious and the unconscious takes place [...] where a "permeability" opens up, "permeability" of the conscious through the unconscious, which makes it possible for the unconscious to be felt much more intensely than in the normal despite repression'.[22]

The relationship between Ferenczi and Hollós was a vibrant one. Ferenczi supported Hollós' professional work, but they differed in one respect: Ferenczi's method started from neurosis and from there down to the narcissistic disorders and pathology. In contrast, Hollós began from the deeper psychological field of psychiatric pathology and tried to reach the everyday life and activity of his patients. Their metapsychological paths often crossed in this decade, culminating in a book jointly published in 1922 as a supplement to the 5th volume of the *Internationale Zeitschrift für Psychoanalyse.* The title was *On the Psychoanalysis of the Paralytic Mental Disorder.*[23] The work, still excellent today, was divided into three parts.[24] The first was Hollós' work on past examples of the relationship between the anatomical body and the psychic processes. The second, also by Hollós, offered detailed case examples. The third, a theoretical one, by Ferenczi, discussed the issues of the interconnection of the physical (the traumatic-real) and the pathological psychological (which is also the fundamental question of Ferenczi's 1924 book, *Thalassa: A Theory of Genitality*).[25]

•

The members of the Budapest School made an ongoing effort to make Freud's works available for the Hungarian-speaking audience. As well as Ferenczi and Vilma Kovács, Hollós also made a valuable contribution to the emergence of the Hungarian technical language of psychoanalysis. From the early 1920s he was engaged in the translation of *Álomfejtés* [*The Interpretation of Dreams*], published in 1935; and *Az Ősvalami és az Én* [*The Ego and the Id*], in 1937. During the translation works, Hollós consulted with Dezső Kosztolányi (1885–1936), celebrated poet, writer, journalist, and translator of his era. In his creative work, Kosztolányi was also inspired by psychoanalytic ideas. Kosztolányi and Hollós shared the project of compiling a Hungarian dictionary of psychoanalytic terms. While this project was not completed, some of the successful attempts they worked on include: consciousness [*Das Bewusstsein*], interpretation [*Deutung*], inhibition [*Hemmung*], Unconscious [*Das Unbewusste*], transference [*Übertangung*].[26]

Among one of the most fascinating extensions of psychoanalytic thought by Hollós is his attempt to formulate a psychoanalytic theory of language, elucidating the instinctual bases of verbal language.[27] The main theoretical frame to examine the development of phonation was the Freudian psychosexual theory. Hollós characterizes sounds as labial-oral, anal, urethral, and genital, according to the dominant libidinal organ of the given developmental phase. Language development itself is interpreted as a kind of sublimation, displacement of the sound production from the libidinal organs to the apparatus of verbal articulation, found beneath the mouth. Parallel with this sublimation process, the sounds get denotations in the mother-child relation, as the mother satisfies the needs of the infant who expresses its frustration by producing sounds. The enthusiasm for Hungarian literature inspired Hollós to apply his 'psychophonetic' theory as an interpretative tool, by preparing statistical counts of the libidinally important sounds (which he calls 'birthmarks') present in prominent Hungarian poetic works, such as the poem *Ode* by Attila József.[28]

What emerges from Hollós' published work and from some of the archival traces he left behind is that he wished for his writings to circulate far and wide, to surpass the confines of both psychiatric and psychoanalytic jargon—ultimately to be accessible in a way that was profoundly open, crossing barriers of education, class, and even language. In a short pamphlet on the theme of alcoholism, published in 1908, he stages a dialogue between a member of the public interested in how to approach alcoholism in everyday life, and a doctor who is answering their questions in a playful but also very informative manner, engaging misconceptions and commonplaces of thought.[29] In a letter to another psychoanalyst of the Budapest School of Psychoanalysis, Vilma Kovács, written in May 1940, Hollós mentions that he would be glad to see his *Yellow House* book translated into English and that a project for such translation had been in place since 1939; he also mentions he has plans to have it translated into French.[30] It was a special event to come across this letter in the spring of 2024, just as the translation into English of the manuscript was being completed. Hollós' wish for a translation into English of his *Farewell to the Yellow House* was granted ninety-seven years after the initial publication in Hungarian and eighty-five years after the first uncompleted project of such a translation. The English volume will now exist alongside the German, French, and Italian translations. [31]

The Hungarian version of the *Farewell* was republished in 1990, one year after the Iron Curtain fell, and the hard dividing walls between the countries of Eastern and Western Europe were removed. The afterword for the 1990 Hungarian edition was written by psychiatrist András Veér, who in 1986 became the director of the National Psychiatric and Neurologic Institute (or Lipótmező, or The Yellow House). In 1988, on the occasion of the 120th anniversary of Lipótmező, András Veér invited an art historian to reinstall the valuable and fragile picture gallery preserved in the asylum. This old psychiatric picture gallery and museum of madness, which was created and opened to the public in 1931, was thus revived.[32] It had survived the dark moments of the twentieth century and had been resting within the walls of the Lipótmező and Angyalföld asylums. This collection of asylum art already offers surprising shifts in perspective: portraits of doctors painted by patient-artists; portraits of patients painted by their fellow patient-artists. It seems that yet another perspective resurfaces from the pages of *My Farewell to the Yellow House*: it is the perspective of the outsider, of the visitor, of the public. Do the gallery of inmate pictures and Hollós' *Farewell* mirror each other? Is there an interaction, a mutual relationship, a triangular arrangement of perspectives? Is there a both textual and pictorial representation of changing viewpoints between the patients, the doctors, and their other—a third who is neither inside nor outside?

In the section called 'The Complaints of a Recovered Patient', Hollós writes: 'The gates of the Yellow House are a fateful meeting place: they divide people at the point where their solidarity should be most apparent.' (p.33). Inviting us to focus on a threshold, Hollós does important and subtle phenomenological work here: he explores a place of being neither inside nor outside, but in between, in a way that nearly substantiates the matter of what separate us. This usually invisible substance—which Hollós works to bring into our consciousness—is the fear of madness.

The preface to the French edition, which we reproduce below, was authored by psychoanalyst Eva Gerő-Brabant. We consider this preface a historical document in its own right. Written in 1986, it functions as a unique 'knot' of transmission of the ideas of the Budapest School of psychoanalysis. Published only one year after the French edition of *The Clinical Diary* of Sándor Ferenczi,[33] translated by the same psychoanalyst who edited the *Diary,* Judith Dupont, the French *Mes adieux à la maison jaune* is part and parcel of a global 'revival' of the Budapest School, which started in the 1980s, and continues in our times. This strong revival came after nearly five decades of traumatic forgetfulness surrounding the work of Sándor Ferenczi and his collaborators and followers. Ferenczi was forgotten after a break with Freud, in 1932, which affected the psychoanalytic field very deeply. The preface by Eva Gerő-Brabant is important because it articulates what until the 1980s had been unspeakable in historicising the Budapest School: its wide-ranging and committed interdisciplinary outlook, or better-said, its porous nature in relation to other fields and discourses, from literature, to anthropology, to the hard sciences; its extraordinary radical voices, including István Hollós, who had strong projects, such as re-socialising madness and breaking down the walls of the asylum; its inclination to social issues, which is also an acknowledgement that psychoanalysis is (or can be) political. We recommend reading Eva Gerő-Brabant's preface alongside our own, as it gives its own useful punctuation of the richness of the Budapest School: it is charged with the unique energy of a moment when something that was not discernible enters our field of perception for the first time and gains shape.

Antal Bókay

Monika Perenyei

Raluca Soreanu

Mónika Takács

Budapest and London, July 2024

Preface:
A Friend of the Insane

István Hollós joined the Hungarian Psychoanalytic Association upon its foundation by Sándor Ferenczi, in 1913. This date marks the *de facto* birth of the psychoanalytic movement in Hungary, where it gained considerable traction despite its late start.

The year 1913 was also a genuine turning point in the history of psychoanalysis in general, when the break between Sigmund Freud and Carl Gustav Jung became both explicit and irreversible. It was now apparent that Freud's attempts to introduce psychoanalysis into the hospital sector had definitely failed.

The ever-delicate relationship between psychiatry and psychoanalysis resembles the personal relationship between Freud and Jung—like the two men, the two disciplines seem fundamentally predisposed to exclude each other.

In 1906, Freud took the initiative to write to the young Swiss psychiatrist to congratulate him on a recently published article. Soon he expressed his wish to bring, through Jung, who meanwhile had become his disciple, "his truth" to the "other world" represented by psychiatric authorities. During the entire span of their friendship, from 1906 to 1913, Freud believed that, when faced with such an assault, his adversaries would simply yield, thus bringing down the barriers between the two disciplines. He was also passionate about this project because of its inseparable link to another: to bring psychoanalysis—the psychoanalytic cause, "la Sache"—out of the Jewish ghetto and transform it into an established and universally recognized science. He thus writes to Jung in 1909: "We are certainly getting ahead; if I am Moses, then you are Joshua and will take possession of the promised land of psychiatry, which I shall only be able to glimpse from afar."[34]

Despite his initial reluctance, Jung eventually accepted the role of Freud's "crown prince" and appeared to embrace "the cause" more fully over time. They carefully avoided points of conflict and began a friendly correspondence primarily focused on their respective research interests and issues arising from their work with patients. However, upon reading these letters, we are inevitably struck by a sense of fundamental misunderstanding, apparent even during the seemingly most harmonious periods of their friendship. Behind the strictly scientific discussions we sense disagreements, which are always hastily stifled. An example of this latent enmity is evident in how each of them theorises their interest in psychosis.[35] Speaking of paranoia, Jung explains that, in his opinion, it is constructed exactly like *dementia praecox*, while Freud writes: "I write paranoia and not Dem. pr. because I regard the former as a good clinical type and the latter as a poor nosographical term."[36]

Jung soon grew tired of his role as a disciple, and, in his quest for independence, he increasingly rejected Freud's influence. In late 1913, the two definitively parted ways. Both experienced this separation as personally painful, yet it also had a decisive influence on the development of their thinking.

As for Freud, he gradually distanced himself from official medicine, as evidenced by advocacy of lay analysis. After the end of their friendship, he also abandoned his attempts to establish dominance in the psychiatric field. He even became openly hostile towards psychiatry. Whilst after Viktor Tausk's suicide he wrote to Lou Andreas-Salomé: "I confess that I do not really miss him", we might wonder if this indifference partially stemmed from the fact that his disciple's research focused on schizophrenia.[37] While continuously trying to expand the field of psychoanalysis, Freud also sought to impose limits on his research. For example, we know how sceptical he was about the efficacy of psychoanalytic treatment for psychotics due to their inability to transfer their affects to the person treating them.

The Hungarian psychoanalytic movement thus began in the same year that Freud started to explicitly distance himself from the medical and psychiatric discourse. Initially, the history of the Hungarian movement was characterised by complete agreement and absolute loyalty to Freud's ideas. During Freud's break with Jung, Ferenczi took a critical stance towards the latter and became a strong advocate for lay analysis. His innovative efforts in terms of the psychoanalytic technique post-1918 also followed Freud's own example, at least at the beginning.

However, starting with Ferenczi, Hungarian analysts slowly began to show a degree of audacity and attempted to explore the "dark continents" of Freudian thought. This development was fuelled not only by the geographical proximity between Vienna and Budapest, but also by the favourable reception of psychoanalysis by the educated Hungarian classes which, while mostly belonging to the radical bourgeoisie, had been deeply disappointed by recent political events. Among others, it should be noted that Hungarian analysts, initially focused primarily on the therapeutic mission, did not shy away from handling so-called difficult cases. This broad clinical experience led them to introduce new perspectives. For example, when Ferenczi sought to study the aetiology of certain neuroses by delving into the pre-Oedipal stage and highlighting the traumatic aspects inherent in the mother-child relationship (while Freud viewed the mother-son relationship as an example of ambivalence), he received a critical letter from Freud. During their subsequent meeting, he also perceived Freud as cold and distant.

Anti-psychiatrist ahead of his time

Hollós, who himself was well aware of the contradictions between psychoanalysis and psychiatry and expressed them by embodying the principles of anti-psychiatry before the term existed, also did not find the support and understanding he had hoped for from Freud.

What do we know about this pioneer of Hungarian psychoanalysis? He was born in 1872 into a Jewish family of modest means. At birth, he was given the name Heszlein, which was not yet "magyarized." He had a sister who also became a psychoanalyst. According to his writings, he had wanted to become a doctor since childhood. He was the first in his family to attend university when he enrolled to study medicine at the Budapest Faculty. He worked as a psychiatrist in various regional hospitals and later was appointed the Director of the country's leading psychiatric clinic in Lipótmező near the capital.

He met Ferenczi in 1905 and the two young men, roughly the same age, quickly became close. From the beginning, Ferenczi assumed the role of guide and theoretician, while Hollós happily embraced the role of disciple and clinician par excellence. We might wonder whether this had something to do with their respective social backgrounds. Ferenczi, whose father was a publisher-bookseller and who had been surrounded by artists, not only had more social fluency but also easier access to the intellectual milieu. Hollós' father was a stonemason.

Besides grappling with financial difficulties, Hollós also encountered challenges in comprehending abstract concepts and had to adapt to a new language distinct from his native tongue, reflecting the common struggle of individuals from working-class backgrounds aspiring to enter the middle class. His unwavering defence of his thesis, which highlights the parallels between the mentally ill and the purportedly sane, also invites reflection on his origins.

It is thus hardly surprising that it was Ferenczi who introduced Hollós to psychoanalysis. Hollós went to visit Freud in Vienna several times, but eventually did his analysis with Paul Federn, who was among the first of Freud's disciples to take an interest in psychosis—no doubt not an unimportant factor in Hollós' later orientation.

We know nothing about the length of his analysis and can only guess based on the average duration of analysis of other pioneers of psychoanalysis. Feeling both the need to educate themselves and continue Freud's work, the first generation of psychoanalysts did not have much time to devote to their personal analyses. According to Jones, Ferenczi's analysis with Freud took place over only two three-week tranches. At the time, Freud would train his disciples while taking a walk with them after completing his long days with patients. Additionally, Ferenczi was the first to emphasise the need for psychoanalysts to undergo personal analysis.

One of the characteristics of the psychoanalytic movement in Hungary was its openness to social issues. Already in 1914 Hollós raised the question of the role society played in the aetiology of the psychoses. In an article published in the literary avant-garde journal *Nyugat* (*The West*), Hollós presented the poetic writings of one of his patients and sought to show the sources of poetic inspiration.[38]

This patient, who was completely unschooled, began his life as an apprentice in a workshop where he was severely abused. Not only did he strive to escape his condition, but he also decided he wanted to become famous. To fulfil his ambitions, he began to attend popular balls, where he distinguished himself as the best dancer—Hollós points out that this was already a manifestation of his interest in rhythmic activities. The patient then decided to become a dance teacher and began to tour small villages where he would rent a space, get the word around and then patiently wait for his students to show up. When his business failed, he decided he hadn't received sufficient training and needed to take lessons with a reputable teacher in England. His lack of money meant he had to undertake the journey on foot; however, he only got as far as France, where he became embroiled in larceny and spent several months in prison. After his expulsion to Hungary, he initially wandered aimlessly for some months but was eventually hospitalised at the psychiatric clinic where Hollós worked. One day, the patient told him he wanted to write poetry and that unless he restrained himself, he could produce verse without interruption. Hollós encouraged him and witnessed the creation of an unexpectedly powerful series of poems. Words, pronounced slowly, were linked together as if by accident, but as they were uttered, they began to form a meaningful whole. Hollós emphasised that the patient had an undeniable talent for poetry, but rather than a poet who had become ill, he had become a poet *because* of his mental illness. For Hollós, the mark of a poet was the ability to remain in close proximity to the unconscious, where he believed the source of poetry lay. His patient thus became a poet because psychosis had opened to him the depths of his unconscious.

However, locating the sources of poetic creation in the poet's unconscious did not make Hollós subscribe to the common belief that artistic talent alone was needed to overcome external obstacles. Plus, at a time when most analysts focused exclusively on individual factors, Hollós showed clearly that he was not oblivious to the impact of social factors on subjective development. "If the force of negative energies of a civilised society is such that it can not only destroy a child's dreams, crush a young man's ambitions, but also reject the most elementary manifestations of his soul, it would be foolish to believe that the power of a developing psyche could defeat that of society." Hollós' article eventually advises the reader: "Skimming these poems and dismissing them as incomprehensible would be an injustice. What we see here is a world of strange thought. To explore its depths, we must acquaint ourselves with this strangeness, just as an ear accustomed to a melody can only appreciate amelodic music after having listened to it repeatedly."

This is a remarkable parallel: the birth of modern music and art, the first scientific research, as well as the beginnings of psychoanalysis did not occur in this turn-of-the-century period by accident. It was a time when, on the one hand, Western thought had lost its belief in its own superiority over others, beginning to be questioned, while, on the other hand, artistic forms previously considered unshakable began to collapse and renew themselves. However, when Hollós tried to understand the psychotic's language, when he published his patient's poems not as symptomatic creations but as literary productions, encouraging his educated and "normal' readers to make an effort to understand them, he was already expressing the perspective on madness that later led him to write *My Farewell to The Yellow House*. By drawing a parallel between the psychotic's language and the new forms of music, Hollós simultaneously demonstrated that he was perfectly aware of being part of a collective current, a genuine cultural revolution of which ideas inspired by psychoanalysis are a part, as well as the blurring of boundaries between the subjective and objective domains in art.

Psychoanalysis, which inspired Hollós' ideas and approach, is itself marked by a double legacy. A descendant of both romanticism and rationalism, it fiercely resists any attempts at categorisation, always transgressing on one side or the other. When it is classified as a science, it is seen as too vague, too intuitive, too subjective; as an art, it is accused of being too rigid and reductive. Freud, for reasons that are quite understandable, mostly emphasised the scientific aspects of his work. Hollós, like practically the entire Hungarian school, was more sensitive to its romantic aspects. When Ferenczi went beyond the limits of strict neutrality, when

Hollós used psychoanalysis to treat psychotics, we are reminded of Lord Byron or Sándor Petőfi who, driven by their romantic sensibility, refused to be confined to the position of a writer.

There are but a few anecdotes about how Hollós ran his clinic, but they deserve to be mentioned because they show his humanistic approach and a remarkable ability to resolve contradictions between his role and his convictions.

A recently hospitalised patient, Mr C., refused to eat, citing his Orthodox Jewish background as the reason for not taking meals at the hospital, where they were not served following the rules of kashrut. Mrs Hollós thus prepared his meals separately, in strict obedience to the rules. One Saturday, she was quite surprised to see her protégé smoking a cigar. When she pointed out to him that the rules of orthodoxy did not just apply to food but also forbade smoking on the day of Shabbat, the patient responded: "Wozu bin ich ein Meschugge?"—"So what's the point of being crazy?"

Soon after, Hollós was called in by the nurses because the same patient managed to snatch a knife from the kitchen and was threatening other patients in the garden. Hollós' simple comment was enough to end the imminent drama: he kindly asked Mr C: "Aber Herr C, sind Sie meschugge?"—"But Mr C, are you crazy?!"

One of Hollas' colleagues recounts the arrival of a young girl to the hospital. She was brought on a stretcher in an emergency. As soon as her restraints were removed, she climbed onto a bench and dived headfirst onto the paved ground. The doctor on call was about to sedate her when Hollós appeared and asked him to wait. He then led the new resident to the agitated ward and sat down next to her. He was speaking to the girl for a long time, while she remained quiet. However, she slowly calmed down and accepted treatment. The sedative was not needed.[39]

In 1925, Hollós was forced to leave his role as the clinic's director because of his Jewish origin. The Horthy regime, which had come into power six years prior, decided that a Jew could not hold such a high position. The rise of antisemitism went hand in hand with chauvinistic propaganda, which the regime used as ideological support. For a few more years, this was a traditional form of antisemitism, based on arguments following a specific logic, namely that Jews were responsible for the two revolutions, as well as the loss of the Hungarian territories in 1918, while simultaneously being oppressive capitalists. The first *numerus clausus* law was decreed in order to bar their access to university, but during this time, and once the so-called period of White Terror had ended, Jews were not yet persecuted in their private lives.

Freud's letter to Hollós

Hollós then decided to focus on his psychoanalytic practice and his activities in the Hungarian Psychoanalytic Association. He became a reputable teacher, training a great number of Hungarian analysts. Edit Gyömörei describes the following episode. Once, when she was threatened by her patient the poet Attila József, greatly agitated and wielding a knife, she managed to stay calm by remembering Hollós' words: "You should never let a patient see you are scared, because when they see your fear, they also become scared and lose all control."[40]

In 1927, after having lost his job, Hollós published *My Farewell to The Yellow House*. This poetic and courageous little book expresses the questions raised by his work as the medical director of a psychiatric ward. In the contemporary psychiatric literature, there is no equivalent to Hollós' highly personal tone: "As soon as I began to understand the language of the patients, I slowly realised that the lunatic asylum and its residents were not what we would like the public opinion to believe... The secret to the common ground between the sick and the healthy began to be revealed to me."

We will see that Hollós did not just settle for this bold beginning, but went all the way in his convictions by defending the mentally ill against the injustice of forced hospitalisation and isolation, and by raising the issue of their reintegration. He concluded that a patient leaving the psychiatric hospital, and seeking to find a place for himself in society, cannot just match the average mental health of someone who has never been institutionalised but must demonstrate a state of mental "superhealth". Some of Hollós' comments show that he was perfectly aware of the social aspects of madness. For example, he points out that intellectual disability can remain unnoticed if the subject is well-to-do and has the financial means to conceal their deficiency. At another time, he points out that while "the question of the mentally ill is just one aspect of a great tangle of social issues", it is a "suitable starting point in the process of unravelling the whole thing." He sees the "poor lunatic" as an unconscious and involuntary martyr, simply protesting against the demands of culture.

At first glance, one has the impression that Hollós sees these "demands of culture" as responsible for mental illness—and we feel inclined to protest against this version of the "noble savage". However, we quickly see that Hollós is more subtle than that. It is true that he primarily blames the "toxicity of sexual repression", but he also questions the hypocrisy of educators, who manage to completely distort the child's ego ideal and orient his behaviour and thought around the "negative heliotrope".

Hollós draws an analogy between the problem of madness and the issue of war. In both cases, we consider ourselves innocent, while blaming "the other" for the events. It is precisely this common hypocritical attitude towards these fundamental issues that perpetuates their existence.

Many of the questions Hollós raises concern the role of the doctor in the psychiatric hospital. Just like Freud, he believes that the choice of medical profession is most often motivated by the fear of illness.

In Hollós' poetic-scientific work, one image brilliantly illustrates the entire drama of his generation of psychoanalysts: one night, meditating in a garden under the starry skies, Hollós feels like he is the only one watching over the world. He understands the task of being a psychoanalyst as having to keep an eye on problems that everyone else prefers to ignore—we may wonder if such a burden is not too much to carry for a single person.

In his book, Hollós boldly tackled the social prejudice against madness. He was nevertheless surprised when the inventor of psychoanalysis admitted he could not quite understand his approach. Having sent a copy of *My Farewell to the Yellow House* (published in German in 1928) to Freud, he received the following reply:

Vienna, October 1928

Dear Doctor

Having been reminded that I'd forgotten to thank you for your recent book, I hope it is not too late to correct this omission. It does not stem from a lack of interest in the topic or the author, whose philanthropic approach I've also come to value. Rather, it was the consequence of unfinished thoughts, which continued to occupy me long after I'd finished reading your book, a reading of an essentially subjective nature.

While I greatly appreciate your warm tone, your understanding and your approach, I found myself in a kind of opposition which was not easy to understand. In the end, I had to admit that the reason was I did not like these patients. Indeed they made me angry. I was irritated by how distant they felt from me and from everything that is human. A surprising intolerance, which makes me rather a bad psychiatrist.

With time, I no longer find myself an interesting subject to analyse, while fully realising this is not an analytically valid argument. Yet, that is precisely why I couldn't delve deeper into explaining this reluctance. Can you understand me better? Am I not behaving like the doctors of the past did towards the hysterics? Could my attitude stem from taking a clearer stance towards the primacy of intellect, the expression of my hostility towards the Id? Or what else?

Please accept, belatedly, my apologies, my thanks and my best regards,

Yours,

Freud

In this letter, Freud indicates, with his usual frankness, his position and his limits. It was probably these very limits that allowed him not just to construct his body of work but also maintain his personal equilibrium. The letter also shows that he did not facilitate the task for those who chose to venture where he himself had decided not to go.

Hollós' friends kept a memory of him as someone who knew how to find joy in everyday life. He had a deep and playful relationship with his wife; their conversations never lacked humour. Mrs Hollós, who had been analysed by Ferenczi, was no doubt able to share her husband's preoccupations. The couple would often spend their Sundays near Lake Balaton, in a small house they had been able to buy. In the evening, you could see Hollós walking in the hills of Buda, sometimes humming popular Hungarian tunes.

In 1933, his life began to darken. Ferenczi's death had a profound impact on him, and he paid him a beautiful tribute in an article published in the medical journal *Gyogyaszat* (*Medical Science*).

Hollós was then elected the president of the Hungarian Psychoanalytic Association, a position he retained until the Association was banned in 1944.

Signs from above

When WWII broke out, Hungary was the ally of the Third Reich. Psychoanalysis was banned, and psychoanalysts increasingly found themselves in dire straits. Soon, there had to be a policeman present during seminars or meetings. Many decided to emigrate. Hollós, no doubt, believed himself to be too old to take on such an adventure. Jews were subject to a series of laws aimed at restricting their activities and later even determining their place of residence.

In March 1944, Hungary was invaded by its ally's forces. From then on, the situation of the country's Jews deteriorated further. Mass deportations began, and certain streets in the capital were closed off, creating a ghetto. In October 1944, Governor Horthy made a desperate attempt to break away from Germany. He failed and the Arrow Cross Party, the Hungarian fascist organisation led by Ferenc Szàlasy, took control. The raids increased in frequency; freshly formed commandos arrested Jews to either deport them or bring them into the ghetto. The way to the ghetto was most precarious: some groups never made it because when they arrived at the banks of Danube, the Arrow Crosses thought it much more practical and faithful to the spirit of national socialism to send them without further ado straight to the bottom of the river. This applied primarily to the elderly and children.

Hollós was seventy-three when he and his wife joined this convoy. We have his account of the events because after the war, having been saved by a miracle, he described them to Paul Federn. The letter deserves to be cited here:[41]

Letter from a survivor

István Hollós to Paul Federn,
17 February 1946

[...]

My wife and I no longer had any chance of escaping death. All the inhabitants of the house protected by the Swedish – nearly two hundred people, men, women, children and the elderly – were transported to the Arrow Crosses headquarters.[42] *On a December night, we were led to the Danube, barefoot, barely clothed. While we awaited our turn for several hours, sixty of us were shot in a side street. And then a miracle happened. All of this remains confused in my mind, despite my attempts to untangle it. All I have is a dream-like image: a freezing and foggy winter night, the silence convulsively interrupted by growls, the glare of searchlights momentarily illuminating the indescribable herd of half-naked people, immobile in the spectral light. This is my only precise memory: we were to follow those ahead of us into death, then stop at a street corner. On our right, the Danube, on our left, the city. A car emerged from the fog. We made a stop. The commander spoke to the car's passengers. It took about five minutes. We were too far away to hear what was said. But it was about Andrassy Avenue. And then we followed the commander to the left, three by three, towards the city, towards life. This column of about a hundred and fifty people snaked through the streets, panting loudly like a gigantic beast. We had narrowly escaped death. They led us back to the cellar and the next day we arrived in the ghetto.*[43]

[...]

I will never forget this terrifying night, facing death on the banks of Danube. A night that forever marked me. Even today, I struggle to understand how, despite all the signs and preparations, none of us wanted to believe what was waiting for us. Yet it was clear: we were going to be shot. Despite all the signs, I hadn't really become aware of what was going to happen to us. My ego had to undergo a profound transformation, erasing the weight of the imminent danger. One of our companions in misery, who had just lost his wife, burst into tears and stumbled out of the ranks. When his son wanted to console him, the two were shot before our eyes. None of this impressed me much; experienced the event as something completely ordinary. Today, this absence of reaction still remains a mystery to me. Because of this ego transformation, our faculty of judgement was distorted to such a degree that we couldn't but trust our executioners. Because they made us believe they were leading us to the ghetto. This metamorphosis of the ego was only a defence, allowing us to reject the unbearable. This defence has nothing to do with scotomization. (One day, I'd like to define the phenomenon). It's important to note that one is conscious of the danger situation. As evidenced by what follows.

At that moment, I was painfully aware I had to leave my son, my sister and my friends. It lasted but a second, but that second felt like eternity. In this sudden collapse of my ego, both paralysed and lucid, I made a quick but profound assessment of my life and, without knowing how, I was engulfed with immense peace. I vividly recall the sign of a laundry shop which I couldn't take my eyes off, constantly rereading the inscription, while humming a tune. At the same time, I felt enveloped by a sense of benevolent peace, which grew stronger minute by minute. I had taken stock and would willingly make my final journey on earth. I was calmly waiting for events to unfold. In this general absence of desire, I only had one: to share my great discovery with my wife as quickly as possible. She too should experience this feeling!

In our procession, the group of men marched ahead of the group of women. I had already tried repeatedly to catch a glimpse of my wife, who was quite far behind me and naturally was trying as best as she could to catch up with me. She managed to do so just as I was experiencing this unique desire. I took her in my arms, looked into her eyes and said calmly: "I've lived for seventy-three years, you've lived for fifty-six, life will have been beautiful." She looked at me with her tranquil eyes and replied with a smile: "Yes, of course, but the water is quite cold." That's where I recognised her, laughter bubbling up from deep within me. She had just reassured me.

Today, I can't imagine this calmness, and even less explain it. We were undoubtedly in a state where one receives signs from above. ...

During the last years of his life, Ferenczi was interested in this feeling of "timeless and spaceless omniscience", felt by a subject who, after a hard struggle, accepts that death is inescapable. What intrigued him was not just that one could voluntarily surrender one's own life, but also that one could "obtain pleasure" from the idea of one's destruction. He speculated that the fact of willingly hastening one's demise relieved anxiety. Ferenczi used the image of a little bird pursued by a bird of prey: at some point, the little bird gives up all resistance and flies towards its enemy's claws. Finally, he described a situation in which such voluntary surrender was followed by compensatory hallucinations combining "deliria of rapture" with a "phantastic identification with the aggressor".[44]

Hollós' letter speaks about a "sudden collapse of [the] ego" and the immense peace that followed. Was this a "compensatory hallucination" or a "state in which one receives signs from above"? Are they speaking about the same thing in two different tongues? While Ferenczi's theories move us because they were developed when he was already suffering from the illness he was to succumb to, revealing his desire to remain lucid until the end, Hollós' testimony touches us on another level. Firstly, we are struck by the absence of analytic terms in his account, aside from the notions of ego transformation and defence, which are useful to his argument. Secondly, there is also a lack of scholarly attitude, as if the events he had witnessed had made the author shed any protective skin, analytical or otherwise. This is precisely how he manages to share his painful near-death experience with us.

I should explain that the miracle that saved Hollós and his wife was named Raoul Wallenberg. The Swedish diplomat spared no effort to save those he could during the persecutions of Jews in Hungary. It was he who, on that night, persuaded the commander of the Arrow Crosses—of course, through bribery—to lead the cohort of Jews to the ghetto rather than to the bottom of the Danube. According to the information spread in Hungary through word of mouth, Wallenberg also ended up disappearing, not in one of Hitler's prisons but in one of Stalin's gulags.

At the end of the war, Hollós thus found himself among the survivors. He then lived through a short period of hope. The Psychoanalytic Association was reconstituted and functioned for three years. Hollós returned to his patients, colleagues and friends; between sessions he would briefly join the salon conversations. Visitors of all kinds often discussed politics. What was exceptional at the time was that the conversation never became a dialogue of the deaf but remained a genuine exchange because, in Hollós' presence, it was impossible to resort to stock phrases. With great lucidity, he patiently listened to the presented ideas, which were still filled with the hope of a classless and problem-free society, and simply reiterated that we should always remain somewhat sceptical of theory, because human beings cannot adapt to theories; rather the latter must be adapted to human beings.

Returning to the Yellow House

The watershed year 1948 marked the end of the period of democratic freedoms in Hungary. The Psychoanalytic Association was banned, and psychoanalytic practice became semi-illegal. Hollós, who had devoted his life to the psychoanalytic movement, couldn't help but feel personally affected by these changes. He found solace in his deep relationships with his wife and friends, which kept him grounded. It is said that during this time, he sketched portraits of his "ancestors" and invented biographies for them. One of these drawings inspired him to write a whole book: *The Unknown Coachman*. In the story, people are connected together by golden threads, which shine above the roads at night.

In 1952, Hollós suffered the loss of his wife. The strongest bond in his life was broken. With the Association disbanded and his ideas deemed socially subversive, he found himself alone and homeless. It's no wonder he began to develop ideas of persecution. Given his circumstances, we might wonder if his delusions were not close to reality. Let's remember that in 1914, a lone human being couldn't indefinitely resist the overwhelming forces outside. Hollós was fully aware of what was happening to him; he confided in his friends that he could "control" his ideas, though it was often exhausting. During a hospitalization at the Angyalföld clinic, he participated in medical staff meetings and continued to assist other patients. By 1955, his mental state improved and he was transferred to Lipótmező —"the Yellow House"—where he was given a private room. However, despite emerging from his psychotic state, he realized his problems remained unchanged. Hollós died in 1957 from pneumonia at the age of eighty-five.

As I have said, in psychoanalysis we find both the influence of romanticism and rationalism. The Budapest School also embodies both tendencies. Imre Hermann, whose research focused on the process of thought, leaned more towards the rationalist side. Conversely, István Hollós, an anti-psychiatrist, represents the romantic trend in both his activities and his theoretical work. He believed that theory should be subject to practice, that it was merely a tool to better understand human beings rather than reducing them to it. A romantic, yet firmly grounded in reality, Hollós often said that if we were unable to love ourselves, we could hardly manage to love others. While a rationalist psychoanalyst might perceive the unconscious as negatively charged, Hollós preferred to highlight its richness and force, constantly marvelling at the different manifestations of the human psyche. One of the paradoxes inherent in his original thought is that while we treat the mentally ill as sick, it is their environment that truly needs "healing".

In *My Farewell to the Yellow House* we witness the emergence of a new conception of madness. This short work is written in simple language with no traces of specialized vocabulary, yet it is in many respects highly complex and instructive. The reader realises that the questions it raises have lost none of their relevance.

At the end of his life, which coincided with the darkest period of Hungarian psychoanalysis, Hollós had lost all hope that his ideas might survive him. He even doubted the efficacy of therapeutic action. He couldn't have foreseen that his ideas would be embraced by posterity and that his name would be remembered by all those fighting for human rights in psychiatry.

Eva Gerő-Brabant, 1986

Translated from French
by Kristina Valendinova
London, 2024

My Farewell to the Yellow House

Dr Telemach Pfeiflein's
Remarkable Writings
On The Liberation Of
The Mentally Ill

Published By

István Hollós

To the reader,

I am passing on the writings of my friend, Doctor Telemach Pfeiflein, to the reader without modification, although the author may have requested I make certain changes. It is my opinion that this is the best means for me to serve the purposes of the creator of the work. All I need ask is for the reader to resist becoming alarmed should this book appear terrifying at first glance as its purpose is to bring clarity and solace to a murky yet fascinating topic.

I do not intend to say any more about Pfeiflein than is revealed in his book. I will only quote two of his favourite turns of phrase:

– No fruit ripens later than man.

And:

– *In Herbis et in Verbis magna Vis est.*
Great strength is contained in plants and words.

May this book demonstrate all this quote conveys of the power of the word.

Dr István Hollós

To professor Freud

Introduction

Dear friend,

When I bade farewell to the house I spent much of my life in, I came across a great many notes among my papers. These notes evoke memories of hours spent in earnest reflection. There was a time when I strained to ease the suffering of others with more passion than experience. Since then, I have grown to appreciate it is no good to eliminate suffering: it too has a life of its own, a birth, and, somewhere in the secret depths of the soul, there is even the insatiable desire for pain. The person who looks sadness in the eye and awaits its natural waning is the better off as, for as long as we live, it is always the times of suffering that die off first, until, of course, they do eventually kill us off.

My contemplations are on occasion strange and even frightening. It is for this reason that I would like you to dress my progeny, unaccustomed to such company, in more fitting garb. With the best of intentions, you are to smuggle in the pain like bitter medicine coated in sugar. I wish for you to take the timid by the hand and lead them, like frightened children, into the secret fog of their destiny.

Because all of us have at some point slumped into a terrifying mire, from which we battled our way into the present at the cost of great suffering and strife. But there is nothing bold about going back from the present.

Yet there were three who dared to return to the fog: the Hero, who did battle with it, the Poet, who wove a story from it, and the insane person, who became lost in it.

We marvel at the first, wonder at the beauty of the second and fear the third, because we have all been heroes and poets, and I know, my friend, that I should express this otherwise, but I am yet to find a word that is fitting but not hurtful... yes we have all been – like the insane.

It is into this great Yellow House that so many who have become lost in the fog will bring the burdens of life for time immeasurable: many of those who mourn fallen loved ones will gaze in this direction with troubled hope. They will bless and curse this house. But sooner or later they will need to understand the house and its inhabitants!

While I sanctified my farewell in a modest celebration, I appended my notes with a good few new thoughts. I'm sending them here, please fashion them into something that may address the predicament of some sufferers and mentally ill.

Written in the pine grove in the autumn of the year of my farewell.

With love,

Your Telemach

1

Tales That Everyone Has Heard

I now wish to tell a tale or two. If you deem it appropriate, commence the work with these.

Once upon a time, a lunatic received a visitor. The nurse left them both for a short time. The lunatic attacked his visitor. He set about strangling him. He commanded that he jump off the upper floor.

Now we must pause. The listener must be left to wait with bated breath.

The visitor is fearful. The lunatic is strong. This is true of every lunatic. At the last moment, the visitor has an idea to save his skin:

"My friend, jumping down is easy. Any child can do it. Just allow me to go down into the courtyard. I will jump up from down there."

The lunatic was pleased with this proposition. Every lunatic believes in the unbelievable.

He sent the visitor on his way without delay. And so he escaped from peril.

This tale is an old memory for me. It is like the first yellow tulip in the garden of the village school. It is through this story that my teacher explained the "presence of the soul". For a long time, this phrase garnered great respect from me. Then the word and its teachings faded and only the lie remained that the good teacher spun.

This tale is a trope: one of a hundred that circulate the globe about the mentally ill.[45] The lunatic strangles people without reason. The lunatic believes in the impossible. He is a lunatic after all.

This tale troubles me greatly. Now I was the one standing face to face with the lunatic. I could not believe he would accept my proposition.

"You are only saying that," he replied in my imagination, "because you think I will believe this nonsense and allow you to escape." And then he continued to strangle me.

But that was not the problem.

The thought processes of my lunatic corresponded to that of a healthy person. My fairy tale was no longer a fairy tale and it was no longer reassuring.

A fairy tale is born of desire...

A lunatic should be different to me! He should be dangerous! She should attack without rhyme or reason! His legs should be made of glass and he should be afraid they will break! If she is a young girl, she should untie her hair as she sings in a wailing, giggling tone of a foetus drowned in water!... Let the lunatic be, for the love of God, a mysterious beast!

Let every tale about the lunatic be the alibi for my own mental health!

There comes a time, however, when we must examine what a lunatic is really like and discover why we should wish to escape from her into the realm of mystical and romantic fantasy.

We are not released from our hidden fears when we flee. Fear flees with us. This is why, my friend, you need to make it clear to anyone who has at last committed to reading these seemingly frightening writings that they must experience a period of restlessness to achieve calm, even if the lunatic is all too similar to the healthy person.

I will share a few notes with you at this point. The first is a letter.

An Old Letter with a Lesson that Never Grows Old

My lady! I ask you to trust me. I know you need support right now. It pains me that you are so gracious to me and plead for my forgiveness so often. who should be begging for forgiveness as I feel very far from justifying the hope held by those who place their trust in me.

In the case of your son, however, I have no cause for hopelessness. I dare to believe he will recover. At your request, it was me who took him in and, as far as was possible under the given circumstances, I made sure his first impression was bearable…

I remain your faithful servant

Doctor Pfeiflein

I must add several comments to this letter. The relatives of patients were so careful in their treatment of me, as a doctor at the Yellow House, that it was an affront to my honour. I always felt the need to steadfastly protest against these outpourings of humility. These voices were saying:

I have heard that the sick are beaten and starved at the asylum. I don't believe that for a second… but… I am trying, kindly, carefully and humbly to convince you, the nurses, the attendants, the clerks, the servants and everyone else to refrain from doing so, not to hurt him or her…

Some use pleasantries to appease the doctor, but there are others who immediately threaten to report him.

On many occasions, relatives of the patient wage the most merciless war against the doctor.

And he often has no choice but to do battle with one hand tied behind his back when he needs them both. He must tolerate the accusation of cruelty when he is sacrificing his life – not just to his ambitions as a doctor, as his efforts are so often entirely in vain, not even to a thirst for knowledge, because most often all his faculties are exhausted in the course of his daily work, but solely because fate brought him to a place where an individual who is locked away and in need of care expects assistance from him and only him in the whole wide world.

How much must a doctor at the Yellow House empathise and forgive in order to continue to work ceaselessly and do so without inflicting new wounds upon those injured persons, even unwittingly.

What else could I have written to this concerned, suspicious mother that she should place her trust in me.

•

I was not even able to write down what I meant when I said I made the first impression of the institution bearable.

The relatives of the patient were in fact informed that the boy was admitted without any significant resistance on account of the dulcet deception that he was being accompanied to see his bride.

There are specialists in hauling people in who boast that, with a little cunning, they are always able to avoid using force on the patient.

Force – or *cunning!*

How many times does this repeat throughout our lives!

They rarely consider that there might be a third way, and that it is the most straightforward:

The truth!

"You are sick and I, as your doctor, believe it is absolutely essential in your own interests to be treated in our institution. Come with me!"

In my experience, patients capable of accepting information, and here we must consider only these individuals, almost always bow to a steadfast statement from the doctor. What is more, there are some who welcome being put in a position where they have no choice. There are others who have long feared finding themselves 'in there'.

Behind the open expression of fear lies a concealed desire.

The compassion applied by means of deception serves the convenience of the environment and not the interests of the patient. I can say from experience that even violence is not as brutal as when the patient is cheated in order to be brought into the institution. Even those in remission are unable to forgive this injury.

If only you were to witness a patient being admitted in this way just once! If you had only seen the way in which the patient enters the office: his expression... the suspicion with which he furtively looks around... the way he turns to the person who accompanied him in...

"But we must go to the railway station..."

He does not understand why everyone is silent, and then he wants to leave.

"Let me go!... My name? Why?"

He looks out in confusion, like someone who does not comprehend what is happening.

"What do you need my watch for? You want to take my knife? But please, where are you taking me?"

And this is the moment when the canny individual who accompanied him in makes himself scarce. The patient chases after him. Strangers block his path in the blink of an eye.

Then the door slams, the one missing the handle that the patient's hands so desperately seek.

It is only after all this that reality jolts through the patient and the terrifying scream is heard:

"They tricked me!"

And what does your Telemach do now? He softens the blow of the first impression...

A Punchline in Service of the Truth

During my time as a medical student, I received a letter from an old teacher of mine in which he informed me that the son of the deputy magistrate had been taken to a mental asylum. The entire county was outraged. Tongues were wagging about how his father had interned the entirely healthy young man for wishing to marry the teacher's daughter. The teacher asked me in the letter to examine the boy and find out how he could be freed.

I visited Balonyai. I brought him face to face with the well-to-do young man. He explained in reasoned fashion how he was tricked into the institution; there was nothing wrong with him – only that his parents were against him, as a rich man, marrying a poor girl. He begged me to free him or he would really go mad among all these madmen.

I was shocked. I could not believe it was possible for someone who spoke so intelligently and knew of everything, who remembered everything and behaved impeccably, to be declared a lunatic dangerous to public health.

I left no stone unturned. I requested the opinions of other doctors, and others still. I wrote, I demanded an inquiry, and made threats until the truth struck home. One day, an article entitled 'A healthy mind in the asylum' was published. The inquiry was launched. For several days, the case was a huge sensation. In time, this too died down. The review came down on the side of the doctors and everything remained as it was.

Tired and bitter, I considered that there exist heartless parents, short-sighted authorities and corrupt doctors after all. After some time, I contacted my teacher. He had given up all hope. His daughter looked at me accusingly.

"And you still want to be a psychiatrist?!"

"Very much so, I want to be a committed combatant for honourable, impartial science," I announced passionately.

•

This is where the punchline of the story should be. You can heap upon this to your heart's content the lesson that, however clearly the truth is proven, there is nothing to ensure we do not remain wedded to the falsehood. There is perhaps an even deeper truth: the difference between knowledge and conviction! As long as we cannot see the deeper truth, perhaps that people need fairy tales, I will not deceive myself that this story will truly bring about conviction.

After many years, I ended up as a doctor in the same asylum to which Balonyai was taken. I found him still there. He was worn and neglected, but he continued to give the impression of the healthy man he once was. He was a little reserved. Initially, he spoke of the childhood years we spent together. He later grew more genial. He once said he wanted to share a secret with me. I had to swear never to tell anyone. He was switched at birth. He became even more genial. When he was a baby, he was taken from the Bécsi Court to the Balonyai house. The real Balonyai baby was smuggled into the royal family. He had noticed some time ago that he was being watched by high-ranking military officers. Later, clear intimations were made in the newspapers. At night, secret voices told him of his family heritage.

All of a sudden, an intricate tapestry of delusions unfolded before me, the threads of which were clearly spun at a very young age.

I had hardly had time to appropriately rectify my past ignorance, or to put my shocking experiences in their proper place, when I returned to speak to my friend one afternoon. I was not even able to greet him; he struck my cheek with all his might.

"Here, you cowardly traitor! Even you have joined my enemies."

In my moment of pain, recollections of every deception I had committed against doctors, authorities and the families of patients ran through me. I felt guilty and knew that what had now occurred was worthy punishment for my past sins.

Whenever I occasionally walked along the acacia avenue of my hometown with acquaintances who asked about the innocent wretch Balonyai, I had the feeling there was no way to drive a deep-rooted and ugly fairy tale from people's souls.

People fell silent in response to my words of explanation. I could read their minds without difficulty:

“This young doctor is already as rotten as all the others.”

Would it not be the only thing of use for Balonyai and his kind to always deliver a striking ‘punchline’ in service of the truth?

Truth and Comedy

A long time ago, a play by Poe set among the mentally ill was being staged at the theatre. In a sanatorium, a curious journalist chances upon a patient who introduces himself as a doctor and accompanies him to see the other patients. Not a single doctor or nurse is present when a storm breaks out. The mentally ill patients, who had been calm up to that point, become enraged and murder the journalist.

The cast of the play came to visit me to observe the patients.

“Gentlemen,” I told my guests, “Your intentions are noble, but your task is thankless. Many actors have portrayed the mentally ill without ever seeing such a person. With great success. If you too wish to achieve acclaim, I advise you to perform your roles as the public desires and according to the instructions of the director: Roll your eyes, tousle your hair, unexpectedly spring up from a state of calm, and unexpectedly collapse following vigorous movement... if you play the lunatic in this way, the audience will gush with enthusiasm. But if you really do manage to learn something here, the audience will ask in bafflement: Which one is mentally ill?

I would have liked to provide tangible proof. I still believed it to be a trifling matter to change people's minds with the truth.

Citing urgent business, I called over Doctor Weissmann to deputise with my guests while I patrolled the ward, and to talk to them about mental illness, treatment and so on.

I returned a quarter of an hour later. My guests were full of praise in recalling Weissmann, who had left to tend to his affairs in the meantime.

"I am delighted," I responded, "that you were satisfied with my deputy. I must admit that you are now in around the same position as that journalist in Poe's piece. The doctor who held forth for you was not only unsound of mind, he was not even a doctor.

"Doctor," one of them asked, "were you not afraid to leave us alone with mental patients?"

"In case a storm were to break out?" another asked, smiling.

"But gentlemen, this many of you can't possibly be afraid of one madman?"

"Yes, yes, but the mentally ill are nonetheless mentally ill, people say they have inhuman strength," the second actor followed up earnestly.

"This is just as much a superstition as the idea that perfectly calm patients fall into a rage during a storm."

My guests surveyed the Yellow House, during which time I introduced Mr Weissmann: the patient.

Prompted by me, he explained that he had been spied upon by secret police all over Europe for many years. They recognised him here, too. They had installed tunnels in the thick walls of the building. From these, they were able to observe his every step, shooting poison at him through fine openings at night. By way of proof, he even knocked on the wall so they too could hear the hollow sound.

I watched the play. The audience was in raptures. The newspapers were full of praise: they had never seen the mentally ill portrayed so naturally. In short, our actors had learned nothing. And when the performers asked my opinion, I did not have the courage to jolt them from their self-satisfaction.

"It was excellent," I said, because it really was excellent. I need to accept that there are always two sides to everything.

Life and stage! Truth and comedy!

There is no use, it is not the rawness of life, but comedy that the audience demands of art.

The trouble begins only when we try to force our dreams upon the realities of life!

A Report on the Madhouse and a Report on the Reporter

I had to tell the same thing to countless reporters that I told the actors. Do not look at anything! The audience demands something else, and what it demands has already been written many times. No winter or spring passes without the same 'Ball at the Asylum', 'Mayday Carnival at the Asylum' and 'Christmas at the Asylum' articles being printed.[46] On more than one occasion, the journalist I had led though the Yellow House was heard to say:

"Nice, very nice, but please, where are the raging lunatics, the straitjackets?"

Yes, a straitjacket! At all costs, for goodness sake, show them a lunatic!

Once, a stern man called upon me to come along now and show him the cellar.

A jocular patient once thrust a thick book under his arm and strode in front of the journalist with a grave face. The visitor asked the patient what he was doing.

"I am Gutenberg, I invented book printing."

"Excellent," the visitor cried out with joy. People's hearts race as they fear and await a miracle. At last, the lunatic spoke: here is the oracle, the mystic.

"Excellent, and what else are you going to invent?"

"Nothing!" the patient replied. "On the contrary, I am going to withdraw my invention so you will not be able to write so much nonsense about us."

The following day, the report was published. It was no different to the others.

The one thing they usually to do for my sake is to write 'mental patient' instead of the word 'lunatic'.

Does the journalist ever consider for a second that his article will be read by the patients? Does the same tact with which he writes about those he feels a responsibility to guide him when it comes to the mentally ill? I imagine that the reporter is on more than one occasion required to sacrifice this tact to sensationalism. He does not consider that the same patient who spoke to him reasonably and amicably would read the following in the newspaper the next day:

A lunatic believes himself to be Gutenberg.

That manic Gutenberg read the report, stroked the paper rose attached to his buttonhole and, with a wry smile, said nothing more than:

"The reporter is not consistent. He interviewed 'patients' and wrote 'madness'."

This was the report submitted by the sick person on the healthy reporter.

About the Straitjacket

The straitjacket is a horrifying thing. So I am often asked to explain what a straitjacket is in actual fact.

No one ever believed that a village judge could tell them more about it than my good self.

Two jurors once brought a patient up from a village by the Danube on a horse-drawn cart. They lifted him off as if he were a sack.

The sturdy man was also wrapped in a fishing net for greater security. Below this, he was swaddled in an item of clothing that was unfamiliar to me at the time. It had sleeves that each ended in ropes, which were tied around his back. I immediately set about releasing him. One of the jurors stepped in:

"Please don't, my dear sir!"

"Why not?"

"It is not permitted, he is a madman and a danger to the public."

"Has he hurt anyone?"

"Oh, please, that the good man hurt anyone, he would not hurt a fly."

"Then why did you tie him up so pitilessly?"

"I ask of you humbly, the esteemed district doctor attests to it that he is a madman who is a danger to himself and the public, it is documented."

"But if he has harmed no one?"

"Yes, I humbly request, we have it on paper

that he is a danger to the public! The reason they have a straitjacket at the parish hall is for it to be put to good use."

This was the first time I had ever seen a straitjacket. I examined it closely so I would be able to tell people what one looked like when asked.

And so to the Nurses

"Yes," I would say in company, "I am sitting here perfectly calm because I know my patients are in good hands. What would my whole profession be worth if I could only trust nurses when looking over their shoulders?!"

For a long time, I believed I would be able to provide my nurses with the inspiration needed for this work, which goes beyond what is humanly possible.

"Impatient," I told them, "is something people out there can be too. This is the difference between nurses and ordinary people. A nurse stops being a nurse when his or her patience runs out."

I did not reckon on it being so different to go among patients with a scientific zeal and healing ambitions than to live among them day and night for the meagre wages of a maid. I believed in the power of my words and encouragement right up until the case of János Magyar came along.

I wish to pay tribute to the memory of

János Magyar on behalf of many patients and in my own name. He was perhaps 20 years old when this simple peasant boy found his way into the Yellow House as a public nurse. He was always patient and conscientious. I sometimes found him awake and off duty as he walked through the ward to stop to talk quietly with a sleepless patient. His patients were clean. He kept their nails and hair in order. There was calm on his ward. When he did his morning rounds, he made his report punctually for all his 50 patients. He was conscientious in following all doctor's orders.

After 15 years of service, János Magyar's mind became muddled, he contracted pneumonia and shortly died.

The fate of János Magyar is, fortunately, not typical. Yet it remains true that, after ten years of service, every nurse should deserve a small village cottage, a carefree life and to never have to see a mental patient again.

But no! It is generally the case that, in addition to this one János Magyar, an assortment of other Jánoses arrive from villages and the far end of the city; unemployed coach drivers and merchants, idle maids and shop hands. They find their way to the Yellow House and – become nurses.

And the Doctors?

"A psychiatrist?! Interesting, let me see. I have never come across a spirited psychiatrist."

"There is something special in his eyes."

"I don't see anything."

"He probably looks upon everyone as crazy."

"He must be very anxious himself."

"On the contrary. He appears very calm."

"He must be jaded."

"Maybe he is just compassionate."

"You only become a madhouse doctor out of humanism."

Here and there, behind his back and before his eyes, thrills large and small flash up. There are some who give him a wide berth, others come to the shrink from far and wide.

And this is how the likes of Telemach Pfeiflein are lumped in with the mental patients.

I used to fight a lot and thought I would eventually get somewhere. Since I have become more careful, however, and this carefulness means, as you know, that I no longer dare to wipe my inky hands in my hair, I have realised that the truth cannot be established on the basis that the other person is in the wrong.

We will also discuss later whether it is really a mistake for a doctor to become a psychiatrist. Certainly, there is a close connection between the doctor and the mental patient. The difference, however, is that:

The patient can recover, but the doctor is never cured. He either dies or has never been a doctor at the Yellow House...

...Now that I am saying good-bye, a 25-year-old memory rises up within me. Coming down from the hill on the far side, the Yellow House suddenly and startlingly emerges shining from the dark forest: a stony crypt placed in an emerald graveyard.

Another Letter

Highly esteemed Member of Parliament!

"...there has been no significant change in your younger brother's condition...

There can be no doubt that the patients demand attention. For the nurses, too..., the nurses need to be trained. Certainly, tending to the body is also important, and, as you are quite right in pointing out, treatment of the patient's mind is particularly so... but it requires a lot of time. But may I be so bold as to also point out that a single psychiatrist is entrusted with the physical and mental well-being of 600 patients. If the doctor only spends one minute with each patient, that makes 600 minutes, or ten hours. A doctor could do his rounds in ten hours if he were to spend one minute with each patient. Will a doctor and those 600 patients be able to cope?!... Perhaps the member of parliament might be able to, etc..."

This letter was written 20 years ago. It is of little solace that a doctor is now assigned half as many patients. It is even less comforting, and this is something I only realised later, that there is little a lawmaker can do even when it is his own brother in the madhouse. The roots of the problems run deeper.

It is with a Heavy Heart that the Sick are Brought in and a Heavy Heart that the Cured are Taken Out

A Transylvanian engineer fell ill aged 40. His illness was serious, his condition only worsened.

One year passed, then another. In the third year, the patient completely turned in on himself, he neither rose from his bed, nor did he speak. By the end of the fifth year, everyone had given up hope. I started work at the Yellow House when the patient was in his eighth year.

In the ninth year, things took an unexpected turn. The patient started taking an interest in the outside world. In the tenth year, he was cured.

The engineer had a wife and adolescent daughter who loved him immensely. When he fell ill, they were desperate. Their pain eased as the years passed; in time, they accepted their fate and what could not be changed. The girl married and the new man assumed the family and business legacy of the father, who was now considered untreatable.

During the course of his recovery, I was able to observe not only the patient, but also his family. The man, who was 50 by that time and at full strength as if revived, looked out upon the world with new vigour and renewed hope. Yet, for the family members, the unanticipated development only opened up long-healed wounds. In the meantime, they had rebuilt their lives in the absence of their father.

At the first signs of improvement, the family was taken aback. Then they were struck down by fearful doubt: can a person really recover if they have been sick for ten years? And there was no denying these doubts concealed a hidden desire: if only things could stay as they were!

The patient really did recover, however. With difficulty, the concerned wife was calmed. The husband was finally able to return to his old kingdom.

The thing they feared came to pass. It was not long before fierce conflict broke out between father and son-in-law. Of course, there was immediately talk of having to intern the father once more. Unfortunately, I know of cases where no other solution is to be found. Here, however, this is not what happened. It was possible to separate the two families. Our man was able to bear the amplified difficulties of being a healed patient with broad shoulders, and he remains steadfast to this day.

The Complaints of a Recovered Patient

A sick person who has recovered should be much healthier than any other mortal.

Anyone can be anxious or else – an individual. A mental patient who has recovered can be neither. All people can see through their blind fear is that the illness has broken out again. They avoid the healed patient. Anyone who has been in the Yellow House is branded. He must keep it a secret or he will not even find work.

Outside the gates, he must be secretive and ashamed.

And there is something dismaying about those who remain outside the gates. They are irrationally afraid of something and someone.

The gates of the Yellow House are a fateful meeting place: they divide people at the point where their solidarity should be most apparent.

•

A patient of mine recovered. He was an upstanding, intelligent man.

While we were playing chess once, he said: I heard you sent Pekarek home.

"Yes."

"Don't let him go!"

"Please, his wife..."

"What about his wife?"

"The woman will chase the man back in no time."

"Then Pekarek cannot be allowed out?"

"He can, but first cure his wife, too."

It appeared that my man was right, Pekarek soon returned.

This chess partner, as I said, had recovered, and as he did not mention it, I brought it up:

"Are you not thinking about going home?"

"Yes, but only for a trial period. I ask that you give me complete freedom to visit home whenever I like."

I immediately granted him permission. A couple of days later, I expressed an interest in him.

"I went home. The first trial was unsuccessful. My wife and daughter were surprised, they were happy to see me and we had a pretty good time. Towards evening, I had some business to attend to at my desk and noticed that the paper knife that was there had disappeared along with the key to the drawer in which my valuables and a rickety revolver were kept. They had hidden them from me. I took this on board in silence: my family had failed the test!"

"And what do you plan to do now?"

"I will take advantage of the doctor's permission and slowly cure my people. I will go home more and more often. I will appear unexpectedly, or stay away when they are expecting me. I will slowly accustom them to this possibility. When I am able to freely come and go, to do this and that, and be angry, temperamental and anxious like anyone else, without people thinking I have gone crazy, that is when I will go home permanently."

And he did just as he had said.

"Of Sound Mind in the Madhouse"

Of course, there are those of sound mind locked up in the asylum. The only unusual thing is that if these people of sound mind leave, society immediately ascertains they are mentally ill.

Take note: the patient is rescued from the Yellow House with the same impatience as that with which he is chased back.

The asylum is a psychological crutch for many people. When leaning upon it, the patient feels fine. He works, goes out and could even be released if he were to receive support in the outside world. But he does not. It is society itself that pitilessly sweeps the legs from under those requiring such moral crutches.

And please note that the same is true in reverse:

A lot of people should be locked up were social privilege, status, wealth and prejudices not to also provide them with an ethical crutch.

"I would release this imbecilic young man," I stated more than once, "but he would have to be placed in a job or position of wealth such that people would not notice he is ill."

•

This event occurred in a small provincial asylum. When I was doing my first rounds, one patient welcomed me with terribly threatening behaviour. For a couple of days, I observed all the excitement in silence.

"I want to leave, you are a scoundrel, you are doing everything just like the other doctor."

"Well now, there is no need for you to be so concerned," I tell him one day, and I call to the nurse to open the door:

"Mister Káhr, you can go."

Two people stood before me, turned to stone: the patient and the nurse.

"I can really leave?" the patient asked in a very hushed tone.

"Any time you wish!" I held the door open for him.

The patient made his way out like a beaten dog; he looked back, repeatedly reached for his hat and disappeared into thin air.

My calculations had not failed me: the patient returned at lunchtime.

On my afternoon rounds, I asked him why he came back.

"This is not a real release," he says a little agitatedly, but politely by now. I should permit him to leave in writing.

I knew that he was a well-intentioned man, but one who just liked to shout. He had been locked up for 15 years and was not afraid to shout: he was not expecting me to have a serious conversation with him.

We discussed that I would release him if he were to receive support from someone for a time. The patient went out regularly. He was sometimes gone for months. In the end, he himself asked me not to force the issue. He did not encounter any person or authority that would help him leave.

Once again, a person of sound mind remained in the Yellow House.

Another Case

This one was as follows:

A man left to his own devices attempted suicide. Although he later recovered in hospital... he ended up on the streets no less destitute. He was thinking of throwing himself under the tram... when a man he had come to know in hospital blocked his path. He clasped his arm and spoke to him at length.

"You have to promise me you will not go through with it. And I will help with your problems soon enough. You don't have anywhere to stay? You will! You haven't eaten for two days? I'll take care of it! I will make sure you don't have to sleep in the grove at winter time. I know how it goes: I tried it myself. But you have to do as I command."

The friend kept talking until the suicidal man walked over to the carriage driver standing on the corner and requested to be taken to see the king.

The carriage driver was bewildered and closely examined the battered exterior of the passenger as he made increasingly loud demands. They were gradually surrounded by a throng of people.

In the meantime, the good friend rushed over to the policeman on the corner. He alerted him that there was a crazed madman on the streets.

The policeman hurried over to the crowd and, seeing the situation unfolding, waved to the carriage driver that he should take them to the lock-up.

Our man was happy that things were going so wonderfully. The next minute, however, he had a fright. At the police station, he would come before a doctor and it would become apparent that it was a ruse. He regretted what he had done.

"Please, sir," he said suddenly, "Please do not take me in, I am not a madman."

The doctor gave a well-intentioned smile. This is what every mental patient says, he thought. Our man recognised the trap he had fallen into and began calmly explaining the situation.

"I went bankrupt, I was starving and no longer had any prospect of making anything of my life. I wanted to kill myself. A friend who had already been in the asylum did everything he could to stop me. He instructed me to say I wanted to see the king. To kick up a fuss. He made me promise. But I can see now that I did not act appropriately. I don't want to pretend – let me go, sir!"

The policemen found the matter strange, but thought better of complicating it.

"No problem," he said, "I will only report that you wanted to go and see the king. The doctor will certainly write the document proving that you are a danger to the public. At least you will have warm accommodation at the Yellow House tonight. Where else would you have to go in this terrible weather?"

Everything was as he said.

It is of no significance here that, during six weeks of observation at the Yellow House, the doctors would speculate on a variety of diagnoses. And as a diagnosis was needed, they found something or other until it perhaps became apparent he was not mentally ill.

What if he really was mentally ill?

But what did he care – the living man – for whom his friend had found a job in the meantime and who was now a proper taxpaying citizen in some provincial town.

"The Heinous Act of a Madman"

A horrifying headline! It shrieks out into the world with its brutal thirst for the sensational... Heinous acts do happen. I too have seen one or two during my long career. But most of the cases they write about are no such thing.

Heinous act: one man murders another. These are crimes also committed by the sane. Sane people carry them out on a grand scale. It's true that they are not referred to as "heinous acts". Instead, these people are "at war".

It is also true that the behaviour of the sane person is motivated: He is killing his enemy.

This is what the mentally ill person does too!

But the lunatic kills imaginary enemies. Sometimes his best friend, parent or child. There is no denying that the difference is huge! But the question does not generally revolve around this difference.

Murder, my friend, is motivated neither by genuine nor imaginary enemies. Deeper forces are at work.

The mentally ill person kills out of self-preservation, fear, revenge, and hatred. The healthy person has a much richer store of motives at his disposal, hundreds of precepts aside from hate that shroud murderous desires behind a veil of good intentions. Our finest precept: watchwords like the happiness of mankind, cultural ideals, truth and even love can all serve to justify killing in their name.

Ideology: a tool that allows man to achieve gratification free of primeval urges, hatred, and pangs of conscience.

Is this idea sick or healthy? It is of no importance, as long as it sufficiently soothes the conscience and conceals that which we wish to conceal.

The "heinous act of the madman" is a cliché. It is written and spoken about as an accessory of the mentally ill.

So how do these "heinous acts" come about?

I'll tell you about one. It was a long time ago.

Morning rounds... A farmer named Dénes repeatedly struck the head doctor with a horseshoe. All I saw were two lines of blood running down to the ground from my boss's broad forehead. Dénes' arms were already held back by the time the head doctor suddenly recoiled and suffocated a scream. While everyone's head was turned, however, another patient, Koncsek, stabbed in the direction of the doctor's stomach with a pocket knife according to a pre-arranged plan. Fortunately, the small knife only pierced his trousers enough to scratch the skin.

The first task for the head doctor was to protect the two attackers from the enraged patients and ensure their safety. Then all he said was:

"It is wonderful that this occurs so rarely. The insane are clearly more patient than the healthy."

At that time, there were more than 600 patients crammed together!

He was the most capable doctor in the house. Tireless and circumspect. Yet he could sense how far out of his depth he was.

"I don't have time," he said, "to be a doctor. I can only be a policeman."

As a policeman – to his credit – he was very bad.

The events were reported in the press.

There was a great outcry. How did a knife find its way into a dangerous patient's hands?! Why don't they ensure stricter supervision?! Why aren't the more seriously ill isolated?! If the nursing staff is insufficient, why don't they take steps to increase its number?!

"We demand a thorough investigation, and we want to know who is responsible!"

Of course: to lock up the insane even more than before. Even more guards, and cells, and straitjackets if necessary! The wild beast must be tied down!

But they never consider that, if 500 healthy people were locked up together, they would commit at least as many heinous acts as the mental patients, if not more.

Indeed, an investigation took place.

"I was unable to ask," complained Dénes, "when that sea of people stood before me in a heap, what I had done to be innocently locked up, and how were those people, to my shame, allowed to work and I was not. Am I not able to hold a spade and a hoe like anyone else? That fellow Bernát came along, and he already knows what life is like here. He said they keep you here for years. And that I am going to die here. You have to beat the head doctor to death, respect has no place as I say. 'Strike him dead!' said that fellow Bernát, and then the truth will finally come out. I did not believe him, but then he brought Koncsek over. I know he has a screw loose, but he does speak some sense. He then said he has a telephone. On it, he heard that the honourable head doctor would not allow my family in. I wanted to ask him why the head doctor wished to destroy me. When I saw once again that I was being neglected and was neither alive nor dead for the sixth month, and nor did I have tobacco, that fellow Bernát shoved this horseshoe into my hand. Whether I live or die, I don't care if they string me up, I thought, what they are doing to me is inhuman. I know I have not behaved well, honourable head doctor sir. Forgive me this one time..."

This is how this heinous act of the mentally ill came about. The mastermind of the heinous act was Bernát.

Dénes regretted what he had done and that nut Koncsek was also remorseful. Only Bernát, the mastermind, continued to retreat into silence and plan further barbarities. Bernát, the world-travelled, half-educated peasant type who litigated via every forum and sought justice and truth in the name of spreading happiness in the world.

The source of many problems lies dormant in the likes of Bernát. They will always find hungry and out-of-work folk like Dénes and exalted monomaniacs like Koncsek, who they are able to exploit for their purposes of making the world a happier place and, when it comes down to it, of aggression.

•

But unfortunate events and accidents do occur in the house that cannot be avoided even with the greatest forethought. But we do have one statistically grounded experience: the more freedom we give patients, the rarer the heinous acts become.

The Storm Corner[47]

Wherever the mentally ill go, a disturbance follows. Doctors, lawmakers, humanists, judges, priests, officials, public servants and guardians of law and order lose their heads, become embittered and heap one mistake upon another at the mere mention of the mentally ill. Everywhere, I heard the same thing: if only the problem of mental illness were not to exist. It is just like the storm corner: you never know what dangers lie in wait.

Matters to do with mental health once had a government official who declared he would oversee the files, but never wanted to see an asylum or a lunatic.

On his travels from village to village, a pedlar married a girl he met along the way. Two days after his wedding, the husband set off on his journey as a pedlar. He never returned.

It so happened that he had become mentally ill at some stage. He was committed to an asylum without anyone knowing. It was only after some time, around two years, that his young wife learned where her husband was.

The woman wanted a divorce from her husband. She was not successful, however. Her family pulled strings at the courthouse, the church, in public service, with doctors and lawyers, but they found no way for the woman to be relieved of her incurable husband, whom she did not really even know. The matter was resolved in the twelfth year. The patient died.

Dawn in the Lock-up

This note from long ago reads like a diary entry.

The wonderful ambience of dawn... I am called to a dying man.

In the half-light at the end of the long corridor, the maniacs sleep in a row, barely visible.

Corridor! Maniac! Cells!

Windowless cells, dark as eye cavities staring into this very moment from centuries gone by.

Cell! Maniac! – when there is no need. None and a hundred times more. Only superstition makes demands that even the brightest sanatorium should have a finely padded, windowless, empty room, filled with straw and with a naked maniac floundering on the floor.

"A cell for the beast! – who is so different to me, he of sound mind."

However modern the Yellow House may be, it still belongs in the middle ages. No amount of cultural veneer will help because the air within the walls of the former prison is growing irate.

Perhaps this is why the lock-up has such a mystical air!

A cool breeze wafts in from the dark gardens. From one cell, snatches of incomprehensible words grind and grind. The rhythmic echo of snoring saws through the silence. The 'maniacs' are asleep in a long row.

The chloral is at work.

Only one patient stirs at the turning of the key, the one waiting on the threshold of the door to be allowed home. He pulls himself up, singing mechanically:

"Come on, let me out now, doctor sir!"

Then, without waiting for my response, he lies back down.

He is the spokesman for the patients who have fallen silent.

Wonderful silent men: maniacs! I saw many of them in the city myself. They were distinguished. I saw them in coffee houses, at the theatre. They performed in the cathedral and in parliament. They bowed down in the shops. They made speeches in the court. And they did this in complete seriousness.

They are no longer distinguished. They are neglected. They groan or giggle in their sleep. Awake, they do not have fits of rage, they are no more than grown men softened into children.

It seems so alien, the way they lie here. What are they doing here? Did they just find their way here by accident? Or was every goal they ever had in life just a prank? And is this genuinely what they want?

As I pace sleepily among the rows of beds, I feel the heavy breathing of a derelict city that has been dragged here.

I am guarding over beautiful people who have fallen into ruin.

I stand in the revivifying cool of dawn like a border post, a frail man all alone. I sense the nocturnal dance of a distant world.

What shall I do with these people who have lain down here with some secret purpose?! What shall I do with those who dance beyond the mountains?!

The dying man has expired. The night nurse shines a light after me in the garden. I am the only one in the world awakening people. I am cold.

As We See It and as They See It

As *we* see it:

Cleanliness! Each morning, the parquet floors are waxed to gleam like mirrors; the brass fittings are polished to shine like gold; the wards glow in the sunlight; the windows sparkle, the furniture has been dusted. The reports are punctually submitted by morning, and, by the time the morning rounds begin, the patients stand in line washed, with their hair combed and their clothes brushed down. Everything is as it should be and runs like clockwork. It took effort and inquiry to establish order, cleanliness and calm... The figures for lung disease and death are down. We provide the patients with work and entertainment. There is a library, there are newspapers, theatre, a chapel...

The food is good and provides the necessary calories... The heating and lighting are adequate... There is even a little love... there is also attention paid to flowers, paintings and good cheer... we can therefore be satisfied with our work.

•

As *they* see it:

"...They brought me in, undressed me,

bathed me, and shaved my hair off with an electric razor. The nurse took me by the arm. I was put in a room. I was admitted there:

"'Here's his data sheet. His shirt and trousers are his own. Half dose."

The dimly lit room smells like a toilet. I was surrounded by a cacophonous noise.

The room attendant sat down, took out a sheet of paper and very slowly entered the details, speaking the words in syllables:

"Dr Antal Gáspár, half dose." Then he looked at me. Then he began consulting with his fellow nurse.

Immediately, the patients came and stood around me in shirts and dressing gowns. They looked at me inquiringly. One of them asked for a cigarette. Another asked me tearfully if I had seen his wife and children; perhaps they had been executed.

"Where should we put Dr Gáspár?" one nurse asked of the other.

Everywhere was full. There must have been 25 or 30 patients in the room. Some were lying on bags of straw between the beds.

"We'll lie Tót down between Berger and Kis," the other nurse said, "they are quiet anyway. Three of them will fit on one bag of straw."

One of the nurses wanted to be particularly considerate and gently put a hand on my arm.

"Let's put Endrei out instead. The corner bed will be better for the doctor. Endrei has epilepsy in any case. He is always falling off the bed. Let him lie on the floor."

So I, the privileged one, was given a bed that I was able to occupy as soon as Endrei had shuffled away.

I sat down on the bed wearily. One or two of my fellows sneaked after me curiously. A small fat man rushed towards me from the far corner, greeting me loudly. His clothes and hat were thrown together from rags in fantastic fashion. He was clutching a package under one arm. He twirled his moustache and pushed the others out of the way.

"Step aside, madhouse denizens," he yelled in a coarse voice. "I greet you, illustrious colleague."

He squeezed my hand, hugging and kissing me. Then he told me everything in a single breath.

"You see, I am János Tatár, master of every branch of medicine, the most healthy man in the world, I put on five kilogrammes a week, I held the front line in the war, I am related to the Habsburgs; I am a poet honoured by Kaiser Wilhelm for my patriotic drama, which was performed on the front to breathe new life into the exhausted troops..."

I listened to János Tatár in a daze.

"Dear colleague," he continued unwaveringly, "don't dismay. You too came here innocent, like me. You are not crazy, you were only locked up here on account of people's jealousy. The troops will arrive to liberate us tomorrow. When we leave, you will be the minister of culture!"

The two nurses were playing cards on the table in the middle of the room. Now and then, they interrupted in mock irritation.

"Tut tut, Mr Tatár, tut tut!..."

This only encouraged Mr Tatár to hold forth once again.

Finally, a tall, pallid patient pushed him away forcefully:

"Go away, Tatár, you have warbled on long enough now, let the clever man get a word in."

Tatár squeezed my hand and squinted his eyes at the lunatic now approaching.

"Dear doctor," my new associate said, "why are you listening to this poor madman?! These are all delusions of grandeur he is bleating about. I'm sorry, Tatár, but I'm going to tell him what's what."

Tatár just squinted.

"Listen to me," he continued in a complaining tone. "Have you ever seen a man without a spinal cord? Well, take a look: I am he."

I listened and listened to the long, monotonous speech, a long-winded story with many names and intricacies.

At last, they rang for dinner. The patients thronged around the table, where the steaming stew was served into everyone's metal pot.

I wanted to escape the incessant racket. I hid my head under the hard pillow.

This is where my nerves will be calmed! Here! This is what my doctor said.

I remember tossing and turning on my bed in despair. A state akin to delirium took me. I was less and less able to understand what had befallen me. It was no longer reality. The red-headed man here at my feet... he occasionally beats his head, and Endrei's spasms – what is this?... And then I am lying on the street. Acquaintances stroll around me and laugh. I wanted to yell out for them to look over here, there is something terrible happening to the red-haired man and Endrei! But they don't see any of it...

This night was as bad as a long, tortuous life.

In the morning, they dressed me in a blue canvas gown. The nurse, keys jangling, led me by the arm to the doctor's office. I was the patient.

A timid-faced doctor greeted me amicably, sat me down and waved to another, who was writing:

"We can begin."

I wanted to cry and beg for mercy, for them to let me go home. It was not possible. The timid-faced doctor asked me to be patient in a gentle but firm tone.

After that, the talk was not about me at all. About someone else: one patient of many whose turn had now come. One question after another in entirely clockwork fashion. My responses only served to prompt the doctor to grasp the structure of the sentences he dictated to his colleague from the ether. Everything I stated became nice, rounded, dictated sentences:

"On request, the patient states his name, age, year and place of birth..."

And so the illnesses I, my parents and relatives had suffered, and whether any of them had been neurotic or mentally ill, had committed suicide or were alcoholics were entered into my medical history. What school I had graduated from. I had to tell the story of my life and, finally, when the House of Árpád died out, when the French revolution took place, how long a metre is, what 3x19 comes to and then I had to repeat the test word after him: Dritteberittenegebirgsartilleriebrigad...[48]

The timid-faced doctor dictated everything. And so I also learned that I was of medium build, medium development and medium nourishment, that my pupils were moderately dilated, equal and respond well, my tendon reflexes can be stimulated, my teeth are notched, my earlobes had grown down and much more that I was no longer able to commit to memory. The doctor took a particularly long time to examine the mucus membrane of my mouth and he showed it to his younger colleague, looked at me meaningfully and clasped my two hands with curious joy because, as he said: it is livid in colour.

I sat before the two doctors like an inventory item that is weighed, prodded and, like so very many things over the centuries, placed on a shelf for no particular reason, just out of habit and with the zeal of blind faith.

The patient navigates space and time well. The doctor paced back and forth and continued to search for sentences in the ether. My fear grew ever greater.

"He responds appropriately to the questions. He remembers the events of the recent past only vaguely. His facial expression is fearful, a little blank, and his behaviour suggests dissimulation. He is in general reserved in his statements."

He said these last words quietly – so I of course listened even more keenly and with bated breath.

I had been taken care of.

The timid-faced doctor asked with satisfaction:

"So, my colleague sir, *quid est*?"

The young doctor was shy and responded bashfully and falteringly:

"If we consider the anamnesis, then we may surmise that the patient has experienced a period of acute disorder."

"Uh, uh," the timid-faced doctor replied, "I wouldn't go as far as to say that."

At every word the head doctor said, I was gripped by troubled trembling.

"The matter is not so simple. This is a more complicated case."

The timid-faced doctor looked at me firmly with his kindly eyes: they pierced my skull.

"There are paranoid tendencies, and indications of dementia, what is more," he felt my skull from right to left, "epileptic elements cannot be ruled out. At first glance, I am tempted to say it is dementia praecox, but... we'll see."[49]

I listened with terrified anticipation. The way he looked! Until then, I had felt I was someone. A teacher. I have students who look up to me. I have friends and acquaintances who respect me. Those two kindly eyes looked through me and I felt that I was now nothing more than a dubious, complicated case. The doctor is counting on his fingers what I might be...

"In the morning report, it said you did not sleep and you tossed and turned restlessly," the young man said.

"Doctor," I said, "yes, please take me out of that room... it is impossible to sleep there... I really will go crazy there..."

The timid-faced doctor furrowed his brow.

"That is not possible," he said, "not yet. The observation is not complete."

From that moment on, I felt a well-meaning but unsolicited omnipotent force hanging over me. My every word and question were weighed up as a symptom of illness. I no longer complained that I could not sleep – because then "the patient is restless". With great care, I managed to be put among the calm patients. Before long, I succumbed to the unforgiving house rules.

Now I was the patient who was roused at five in the morning, bathed with the other patients in the washing area beside the lavatory, dried down with a communal sheet; fed egg soup out of a metal pot; I was not allowed to keep matches or a knife on me, but I had to carry around my comb, soap and bread in my pockets.

My days passed in waiting and idleness...

It is a terrible thing to stand behind locked doors and to wait and wait, and to spy through barred windows in the hope that something or someone will come. And nothing ever comes, and no one ever comes. The biggest event of the day is when the doctor does his rounds. This is a long-awaited moment, even though I knew it too would never yield anything new. The doctor is surrounded by 10-20 patients at once and I was happy, despite having so much to say, just to be granted permission to write letters. During the visit, the patients become agitated, a hundred of them asking for a hundred different things. There were many insane things, but also many that were reasonable. And the doctor on his rounds is always in a rush. I don't know if the patients are always agitated because the doctor is in a rush, of if the doctor is rushing to keep the patients calm.

Ultimately, what more can I expect from life?! I am the lunatic who will be looked upon with oblique suspicion, behind whose back they will laugh. What will my students say? Will I be able to go among the children like someone returning from a sanatorium for pulmonary complaints? Am I right to hope for my release under these circumstances?...

Flowers Among the Rocks...

The Yellow House has a unique atmosphere.

Amid the stillness and quiet of its surroundings, the house with its eternal monotonous rumble takes refuge like a fearsome secret...

The Yellow House has a unique atmosphere. It has musty crannies. Yellowed, dusty writings disintegrate in the doctors' rooms. Inside cupboards with glass doors that open unwillingly, instruments, glass cups, vein strippers, syringes, cranial compasses and primitive microscopes decay into rust. Behind the curtains left to sag in the ceremonial room hangs a picture of him-on-high; surrounded by portraits of former doctors looking down sternly in their black attilas.[50]

The House has a unique atmosphere. Odd people dressed in odd clothing of times passed. They recall deceased doctors... By a warm cocklestove on a winter morning, they sit down to play cards amid clouds of pipe smoke. They recount Christmases long ago. Then every patient received new clothes; meerschaum pipes, tobacco pouches. They tell the story of how the Greek safe-cracker broke out of his cell in '80, and then struck down the night guard... When a measure of wine cost seven kreuzers...[51]

The small, separate rooms also have a unique atmosphere... Miss Janka's room... A birdcage in white muslin. She is herself white-haired and with a wrinkled face, but she smiles childishly with her violet-blue eyes... Her dress is white, pinned fustian, and her fine fingers are like porcelain in her white knitted gloves... The tiny, garish tables, tablecloths, dolls, toy carts, court carriages, cradles and even coffins she made herself out of walnut shells, matchboxes, pictures cut out of old newspapers, glass stoppers, beads, rags, pieces of cotton, feathers... And all these have their own stories... worldly stories.

"Ja, das ist der Wagen Kaiser Maximilians... Dort ist der arme Rudolf in seiner Gruft ..."[52]

Sometimes, the sound of a piano can be heard coming from the men's ward. Everyone knows the mute patient who has been here as long as Miss Janka. After lunch, he always plays *The Virgin's Prayer*. His playing is like a warm and quiet summer shower... It is a confession of love that has lasted decades – from a distance. Miss Janka smiles sweetly and silently nods at me:

"Oh, the lunatic!"[53]

And in the nooks of the rooms lies an old bible here and a Montepin or Dumas novel there, and a volume of *Gartenlaube* from the last century.[54]

The creaky, heavy oak gate under their arches where so many people have entered – and indeed so few left – have a unique atmosphere... The older patients motion dismissively:

"I too will only be leaving this place through the back gate: when old Hubner takes me out."

Hubner had a flat beneath the woods, adjacent to the Yellow House's autopsy building and funeral home. He took care of the dead. He was a quiet man. Without a word, he would take the corpses out to his house. Until he once lost his mind. The patients convinced him that he had fallen in love with the dead and made merry with them at night.

The front porter found his way here from the Bach era and Moravia.[55] The good old fellow would gently knock on the door of the inspection doctors when a patient was admitted at night and apologetically utter:

"They brought one in!"

On summer evenings, we, doctors and clerks, would sit out, as is the habit in a village, on the little bench under the gate and the old fellow would start telling stories about the old days with great reverence. The good old days! When the respected Masznyik head doctor still rode out into the Mátyás Woods on horseback every morning... On Sunday, the gentlemen would come out in carriages and dance on the meadow alongside the gypsies... And it was a folk holiday, with ox roasted on a spit. Once, when it was still

7 in the morning, two dames arrived, their carriage must have stood somewhere outside...

"I did not know who they were, I was just brushing the attila and the patient was sweeping up," he recounted further, "and, all of a sudden, I thought something was troubling him because he saluted them with the broom and exclaimed:

"Gewehr heraus!"[56]

"Well, the patient recognised it was Ihre Majestät with the court lady: she just happened to be taking her for a morning carriage ride, and wanted to take a look at the lunatics."[57]

There is one patient who lost his sight over time. He cheerfully bumbles around and knows the nooks and crannies of the Yellow House better than we do. He once told his story:

"I was not a completely mad, just a little confused. My wife fed the doctor all manner of things, but I knew what she was saying, she also claimed I attacked her with a knife, but it was all a lie. Of course, she was not entirely good-hearted towards me because of, dear doctor sir, the other one, her partner, with whom she was on good terms... the man. If she had been good of heart, she would have got me out. She once came here and wanted to kiss me, I told her: never kiss me if you don't want to take me out... I never go back on my word, I told her not to come any more then... And she didn't come from that moment on... Then time passed... It was hard without my good woman..."

"Difficult... I can't say I have been with a woman since I've been here, and I do not deny to the redoubtable doctor that I have given up hope because, if I should commit such madness as to make advances on a girl, I would never be released... And so the time passed from day to day, week to week, month to month, year to year... so I gave it up..."

Wonderful life stories...

Incomprehensible people. The stone walls are only a perimeter for this social group without a society, a possible destiny made up of individuals who will never belong together... People were gathered here, perhaps because the table of contents of a great book entitled *Psychiatry* put them all under one roof... They build a system around the various forms of illness – paranoia, paralysis, dementia praecox, imbecility, alcoholism, epileptic, manic and depressive mental disorders, and so on. But for the love of God, this means people with different needs, and the different requirements associated with their conditions and healing, are locked behind the same bars!

It is as if the fragments and layers of an upturned world have been thrown together here.

It is an incredibly jumbled social group, one without a society.

Yet life is able to build bridges between even the starkest of contrasts.

Two elderly men, one skinny, the other

squat. One is wearing a long redingote that already has a green sheen. He was once a high-ranking official. The other was a carpenter: he is wearing the coarse baize coat of the institution. The official continuously speaks at length, the carpenter responds in brief. The official asks about the universe and the planets, the carpenter nods understandingly and discusses "manufacturing and the sideboard".

They address one another informally. Any differences in rank between them have long since been eroded by time, necessity, mutual dependence and the illness through which they have nursed each other.

It was astonishing how these two men came to an understanding in their two different tongues.

A wonderful duet! One played Bach on the violin, the other a waltz on the accordion... And yet the two melodies were somehow able to interact.

My friend, speech is a bridge, but the bridge becomes unnecessary when the river recedes below it and people cross its bed to meet.

...On Sundays, the summer brings day-trippers from the city flooding over.

Many of them stop and stare in through the fence. A frightened woman holds her husband close. Then she looks at me, then her husband looks at me too. Then they look at each other and at me again. They both stare at me.

Their silent dialogue is familiar to me.

"Who would think," they say, "that he is crazy too!?"

"My friends," I want to tell them, "Do not be afraid of me, and do not be surprised by me. Even if you happened to be right, this would still create a dividing wall of the kind that I now see between us: the lunatic here, the healthy person there, but in truth there is nothing between one person and the next."

Procession to Calvary

The park is at its most striking from three to five in the afternoon.

Like big-headed animals, they look beneath the thick branches at the yellow, winding roads on which parents, children, fathers, husbands, wives, brides, friends and lovers make their way up in throngs:

The patients and their sick.[58]

They stand in line outside the door of the duty doctor. They request permission to visit their loved ones. They ask for information on the condition of the patient. They crave a word of reassurance.

Much bitter torment converges there.

"Is our brother here?" three of them ask at once.

"This is treachery! We attest that he is healthy! There's nothing wrong with him! His wife had him locked up so she could continue her easy life undisturbed."

I have no way of calming these agitated people. The wife had been suffering the deterioration of her husband's mind in secret for years, even as he went about his business without revealing any abnormality to his friends and relatives by day. At home, however, and mainly at night, he was agitated and caused a scene. Eventually, he threatened to kill his wife and children. When the lady consulted a doctor, he immediately had him taken to a closed institution on the grounds he was a danger to himself and the public. For years, the wife suffered as a martyr – during which time the brothers did nothing for the patient. Now, in addition to this severe blow, the woman must also bear the terrible and increasingly obdurate accusation that she wishes to do away with her husband.

The parents come and beg, they beg: I wish I could tell their daughter that her groom is incurable to prevent the bride from withering in the city. This is what I should say – for what would he be worth even if he were cured.

I should not allow in the friends who destroyed the boy.

Then a lady arrives excitedly.

"Doctor, sir, what is the person who does not leave my husband alone even here doing in this place? She was the one who destroyed him. She seduced him. Doctor, I prohibit her from visiting my husband."

Immediately, another woman enters.

"You want to bar *me* from seeing my poor sick man?! I, who am everything to him, and he who is the father to my children; until we were struck down by this calamity, we lived happily, and only that woman disturbed our peace. She was the one who turned this man into a wretch. Please, do not allow her in!..."

"But, my lady," I say, "She is the patient's wedded wife."

"Yes, it is true, his wedded wife, but doctor," in saying this she proudly stands up straight, "He lived with me!"

And then there are husbands, wives, close and distant relatives curious to know when the patient will die. Sometimes, I could not hold myself back from answering:

"I do not know. What is more, it is not even certain that he is the one who will die first among us." I was able to read from the surprised faces:

"Wicked man!"

•

And when the women want to kiss the hands of the doctor!

"Tell me, my good doctor, is my darling, my only son, sick? Why was he struck down by this terrible illness? Even last week (and here she bursts into tears), even last week, we did not notice anything amiss with him. My darling was so good-humoured, so sweet; but he will be cured, won't he?! Tell me, my only good doctor, I beg you with palms pressed together to tell me: he will be cured, won't he?!"

How many times has your Telemach, so long hardened by the flames of anguish, looked into these tearful eyes, and how many times did he nonetheless have to hopelessly nod so that those begging for reassurance by such means of blackmail should receive it – if only for a moment.

The mothers come. At first, every day. Then, as life allows them to... They toil their way upwards bringing packages, bags, baskets, food, a little soup, pillows, clothes, books, and stationary.

"I brought a letter from his friend, please grant your permission, my dear doctor, maybe it will do some good."

"It was so good today, he spoke so well. It does him good when I visit. He asked about everything. I can come every day, can't I?"

"My poor, dear son spat on me today, he was very agitated. So I won't come for a while."

And the day after tomorrow, she is standing at my door again.

If they are not allowed in, they ask the nurse, the sister, the other patients. Sometimes, they hang around for hours hoping to catch a glimpse through a fence or window.

They come for years, they wither before their time. They worry, hope, cry and suffer; all of them worn down into people that are one and the same. They arrange to come at the same time. They harass or praise the attendants, doctors and nurses as one, and they console one another.

"My son kissed me today. What about yours?"

"The doctor didn't let me see him. He said they had to put him in the ward for disturbed patients."

"Well, God will come to your aid too one day. Look, he said the same thing to me last week. I couldn't visit him then. But he let me in today and it was good."

They became so humble. This suffices as a gift from God. Then they go to churches and pilgrimage sites. In secret, they hang amulets around the neck of the patient. They bring medicine women. They cut out sensational reports about cures for mental illness from newspapers and bring them to the doctors... Please try it! Who could ever be insulted by them?!

And they come in winter, tireless through the freeze. A funeral procession making a pilgrimage to dead who may rise again...

Mourners who prefer to deny their dead!

They do not speak of their children who end up in the Yellow House. They keep it secret. They ask the doctor not to tell anyone for all the world!

"He was in a sanatorium until now, but we can no longer bear the considerable cost. The problem is enough in itself. Why would the Yellow House do any more harm to our brothers and sisters?"

The funeral procession is accompanied by shame and embarrassment.

"I was always very proud of my son. Now I avoid people so they don't ask after him."

"He would be better off dead!"

•

These are the last reverberations of great struggles past. It began perhaps when the child repeatedly broke free of the mother – from her womb and her breast... The mentally ill turn back towards an infinite sea of mist, where the outline of a soul condensed to take form is finely woven. The child broke free for nothing! Yet we remain connected to the mother by a million veins even after birth... A past full of life that runs into the mother's womb like tiny blood vessels and is now torn apart along with all the buds and branches of life. During a breakdown, fantastic energies, expressions of love and accumulations of hatred are freed up and crash down on the mother...

Every step the mother takes to get here is a procession to Calvary.

Together on the Road to Calvary

My friend, everyone looks towards Calvary in fear because ancient, medieval struggles still echo through people. It is because of these that they grow agitated, and become hurried, disturbed and panicked.

I wanted to free Balonyai from the Yellow House and I made serious accusations against his parents, officials and doctors. Today, people in their thousands continue to be engaged in this tortuous and fruitless struggle.

The reporter writes about the patient as demanded by the exaggerated fantasies of the populace. Overly sensitive people free the patient because they are in a panic that they have locked up the wrong person, while the same people also chase the cured patient back in because they are stricken by fear of the patient and for their own safety.

Public opinion is scandalised if a lunatic is allowed onto the street, but people are nonchalant in their tolerance of the hundreds and hundreds of patients crowded together under the supervision of just a few doctors and nurses.

Authorities, judges, doctors and lawyers grow hesitant and uncertain when a case of mental illness is to be discussed.

We Telemachs believe they are wrong even as they cannot allow themselves to believe what we are saying about mental patients.

Perhaps we are wrong too!

We too have no way of knowing the truth about the Yellow House, and about the mental patient. We too are deceiving ourselves. In reality, only the mental patient knows what he or she is.

As soon as I began to understand the language of the patients, I slowly realised that the lunatic asylum and its residents were not what we would like public opinion to believe... The secret to the common ground between the sick and the healthy began to be revealed to me.

The Yellow House: the mysterious fog.

And the mental patient?

"*Tat tvam asi*![59] That art thou!"

2

What Not Everyone Knows About the Mentally Ill

Let us then talk about those we refer to as mentally ill. Those about whom everyone has their own opinion:

Lunatic!

When he roams the village: lunatic! When he is in the sanatorium: patient. When he is locked up: he was put in the lunatic asylum. When he comes out, he is embarrassed to admit: I was in an institution.

Mental patient: discretion with regard to the patient – and to the mother.

It will not be easy to navigate the forest of untruths.

I spent a long time mulling over where I would find the main thread of what I had to say. Suddenly, I became aware of being pursued by a line of verse. When something whispers in your ear unsolicited and unnoticed, you know it is of significance. If you are being pursued by an aria, find the text and you may discover it is related to whatever is occupying you at the time. I grasped the line that was constantly recurring: it was from the Berzsenyi poem 'My Arrival in Harbour'.[60] And there it was, the core of my message was to be found in this line. The title of my next note, therefore, is:

I Take Down my Sails

A dear young friend was the hero of my story. He set off into the world with excellent intellectual and physical characteristics and great enthusiasm. Everyone loved him and predicted he would have a bright future.

For his mother's part, she expected him to compensate her for all the suffering of life.

A horrific event upturned every hope the young man had. He was severely burned. His pretty face was contorted by scars and now induced disgust, his hearing and speech were ruined.

My poor friend, who was connected to the world by a million threads and was met with flattery everywhere he went, now only encountered pity. From people's greetings to the well-intentioned comforting of his friends, he was struck down by millions upon millions of tiny changes.

Life took on a completely new form. It was as if it were not he but the world that had changed.

The girl he loved left him without a word.

My friend was inconsolable. At first, he fought to regain his lost riches but he soon realised it was all in vain. He severed all connections: he avoided friends and acquaintances and abandoned his studies; you might say he withdrew.

We can only withdraw if we have gone forth at some time. What is it that follows these pathways, or makes us follow them?

My friend, I should say a few words at this point about this commonplace and apparently meaningless matter – a person withdrew. It would take us forward greatly and also be of considerable scientific value. And I have a cautious respect for science. All I want to say here is that whatever causes this withdrawal bears some relation to the feeling of love; it is something that enables a person to connect with the outside world. Perhaps this question will become clearer later. For now, I will just say it is from this something that a withdrawal originates.

It is sometimes a tragic path!

This path generally equates to loneliness and the avoidance of company. This is the path travelled by mourning. But individuals living in a healthy environment also seek and find solace in withdrawal, in solitude: in nature, in travel, in books, in studies. Sometimes, however, a person is not capable even of this. In such cases, unrelenting withdrawal may lead to mental illness.

The young man repeatedly made efforts to pull himself out of this fatal vortex. He was impatient, his innocence tormented him, and he would have liked to have something to hold onto, but he could feel there was nothing.

"It was easy for Euler, the mathematician," he once said, "he went blind in old age, or for Helen Keller, who was born mute and without sight. The truth is neither of them were tormented by a sense of betrayal."

For a time, his impatience was so great that he was not able to stay at home for even a minute and spent days roaming the suburbs to avoid any acquaintances. He would say with bitterness:

"I am like a dog chased away into a foreign land, I will never find my owner."

After some time, he grew calm. He sat around at home instead. But he was afraid of all kinds of illness. Someone who had previously yearned for death now observed himself with careful attention to detail. He was terrified of pneumonia. I repeatedly had to examine him for various diseases.

"What happened?"

The withdrawal from the outside world into the self had reached the first way-point, the body. With this newfound curiosity, the terrible tension dissipated, and the sufferer grew more patient.

The patient now visited me more frequently. I had a sick servant who was simply radiant with happiness. He always talked about how not even the director issues orders to him. They had already dismissed four because of him. Now he himself will be director.

My friend looked at the servant without a word for a long while. A tear rolled down his scarred face and he said:

"If only I were as far along as he is."

All of a sudden, I noticed my friend looking out in front of him in a troubled fashion for moments at a time. He spoke of gardens and his sweetheart before suddenly returning to his senses without knowing what had befallen him. This was how the poor fellow was able to break free from reality and create for himself through hallucination a world that reality had denied him.

This was, however, only dreamlike escapism. He still had to wake up. But the struggle had already tipped in favour of a return.

The patient grew quieter, sat in one place and did not eat. He refused contact with his mother.

One night, I was awoken to be told they had brought him in. I don't know what was stirring in his soul at that time. He was wordless and stared out in front of himself. Just from the way he pulled the blanket over his head, I suspected he had arrived at his destination.

•

This story does not sound particularly scientific. It has a strong taste of the romantic. It speaks both for us and against us that this is how thinkers conceived the origins of mental illness until the middle of the last century. The origin of illness – they said – is betrayal. We know today that people do not fall ill simply from betrayal. And yet there is also some truth in the old school of thought. Betrayal accumulates the love that is held back. The healthy person is able to direct the high water accumulated in this way towards loftier goals.

Only where the personality has been injured at some point during the development process in childhood – something on which I will say more later – a hidden sediment rises up, due to which the flood of love is barely able or entirely unable to swell in such a way. In the case of our patient, he is certain to have already suffered such a trauma in childhood.

•

The sad play had one more act remaining.

The patient began talking to himself. He did not acknowledge his family members. His fragmented speech only revealed that he lived in a country known as Territo, of which he was the leader on high. He quietly issued orders. He packed his world ever more densely and created people and fought and won wars using incomprehensible words he considered to be magical. The veil of delusions was however not yet thick enough to prevent the reality of life from glinting through it nonetheless. When his mother visited, he stared out in front of himself without a word, but the tears welling up in his eyes revealed that his attempts to appear estranged were in vain. In reality, he was not. Following another visit, he demanded with vehemence for "his soldiers" to lead that "lady" away. Then he fell into bed, curled up and from then on became stiff and silent. He entered into the state in which the sensory organs shut down and the impulses to move cease. It became necessary to feed him and attend to his needs as if he were a child. He no longer felt the need to fight. He sank into the place where not even the sounds of the realities of life can be heard: the most ancient depths of his self.

•

Mental illness: withdrawal.

I said in my introductory lines that we have all been heroes, poets and mentally ill. I am now able to express myself more clearly. Everyone has lived an archaic time in their childhood, complete with the wonderful omnipotence and hallucinatory gratification of desires to be God, king and hero... *Anyone able to realise this dream: that is the hero. Then there is the person able to express it: that is the poet. And the person who returns to it permanently: that is the mentally ill person.*

And so we all have considerable common ground with the mentally ill:

The place to which those who have been disappointed wish to return is that from which the lust for life drives us towards reality. We all glance back anxiously at the seductive abyss. This is our nirvana and our Calvary.

With his jumbled words, the mental patient stirs up our own haunting past. This is why we are appalled by him. *This is why the lunatic is both a prophet and a saint, at the sight of whom the frightening spectre of our omnipotence and insignificance rears up.*

Mental illness is not possession by the devil.

Those who are sick and those who are healthy both carry the past around within them. Before them is the inexorable reality, behind them their former hallucinatory omnipotence. In moments of crisis, so many of us feel the desire to let go of the bindings of reality and to slip down, back... And in the end, everyone can say:

I have come to shore, I take down my sails...
Peace is now with me: I moor my boat,
Oh, secluded berth, take into your bosom
The ardent youth.[61]

Dániel Berzsenyi

•

I know, my friend, that my explanation raises many doubts. But I do not also undertake to allay uncertainty when my goal is nothing more than to shine a light on certain calamitous prejudices and to leave the thinker to ponder. And so it is also of no interest to me that I do not appear scientific. When the patient entered the doctor's office, the sea of knowledge looked right through the poor wretch just as the philanthropist full of plans to make the world a happier place cannot see a man starving before his eyes.

I had much to forget about science before I could learn to understand what the patient is saying in his own distorted tongue. Since then, Telemach has yearned to know *where these stammering people come from, where they are going and what they want.*

Around the Source

I told the sad story of how my friend relinquished his ties to reality and allowed his self to drift back to the former realm of hallucinatory wonders. I now wish to reveal the huge effort with which this son of man fought his way up from the world of wonders into the world of reality.

For a while, he did not need to wake up. What happens in the mother's womb before the birth of man we barely know anything about. We do know, however, that birth is the first reality to which human beings wake up, and how dramatic it is. And the battle starts even then: between the desire to return to the dream and the awakening to the reality that disturbs it. Thus arises the wisdom of the east:

"It is better to stand than to walk, it is better to lie than to stand, it is better to sit than to stand, it is better to stand, to sleep, to dream, to die..."

The infant desires to return. Soothing silence and peace were interrupted by the trauma of birth, breathlessness and cold, and so the infant instinctively seeks its lost tranquillity: it cries. Those caring for it create a warm, soft, dark and quiet world much like the old one, in which the newborn slumbers once more.

The infant is omnipotent! She cried and her old, undisturbed world returned.

People tiptoe around her as if they can sense she has arrived in that unknown world of wonder.

And that which reaches her of reality, light and sound, hovers merely as a murky fog over a soul immersed in calm.

"And day after day, like a single day...

The pendulum of life swings uneasily. The tiny being has sunk entirely into her almost silent heartbeat. But what is always present: the dream, the fog, shapeless dream fragments, the dust-cloud of dreams that dances at her beck and call, a dizzying, creeping vortex bringing laughter or horror. Screams, moving shadows, distorted figures, pains, fears, laughter, dreaming, dreams... everything is a single dream, by day as at night... and the light of friendly eyes amid the chaos; a flood of joy that pours forth from the mother's body, from breasts swollen with milk, into her body."

So wrote the author of *Jean-Christophe*. The infant is omnipotent. Romain Rolland later speaks of a force.

"...the force that is within her, the terrifying force that accumulates, the warring ocean that swells entrapped within the body of this small child...

...anyone able to read into it would see worlds half buried in the haze, patches of fog that drift together, a universe in the making. Her being is boundless: everything in existence is she."[62]

What is this boundless force?

One that swells entrapped and the other that keeps it entrapped?

The warring ocean? Yes, my friend, I now must tell you in short: the sexual instincts. And the force that restrains them? The self-preservation instincts.

It would have been easier to refer to the two forces by their old, familiar names:

The species- and self-preservation instincts. But these two names are, for our concepts – narrow.

We are All Born Caesars

I now return to the Yellow House.

The autumn fog casts unassuming veils among the crowns of the trees. In the valley, the castle-like towers of the Yellow House now glow towards the heavens with the devotion of interlocking hands.

I rejoice.

The ocean of thousands of years of suffering at the lunatic asylum rumbles monotonously. The screams of the cave-dweller, the prayers of prehistoric man, the wailing of Oedipus, the terrified yells of persecuted medieval man all converge here.

As I listened for decades to the woes of mankind, I became removed from life's reality. I know little more of the distant city than that it is where people struggle, fighting for better and for worse, and that three from among them will wash up in the Yellow House every day.

Yes, my friend, Franci comes to mind: I asked him on the occasion of his 40-year 'jubilee':

"Are you going into town? The world has changed greatly in 40 years!"

"Doctor, sir, I will not go. It is a very treacherous place, read about it in the papers. So many people commit suicide there, I may even catch a stray shot.

Telemach sees the practical side of life from a single perspective, just like Franci.

And yet it is the Telemachs of this world who have something to say to life's people.

Because the Telemachs conduct secret conversations with those who know life all too well, those who were crippled by it.

I had a patient, Caesar Cadavi, of whom I have much to say, and who said of a dark winter afternoon:

"We are all born Caesars."

There are some people who realise their grandiose childhood fantasies in life. These are the rarest: They remain Caesars.

There are those, the majority, who strike a compromise with life.

And those who break down in this struggle.

•

Yes, for those who break down, the science says they are weak: they were weighed down.

We are accustomed to answering unanswerable questions with words. One such word is 'hereditary'. It is a good way of putting our sense of inadequacy to sleep.

There can be no doubt that our life path has deep roots in a past prior to birth. But there is a root that goes unnoticed, the one in life after birth, in childhood.

Any farmer understands that the greatest threat to a rich harvest is an early frost.

•

As much as it pains me, my friend, I must also speak of things that are labelled scientific; but I do not do so in the interests of science. I have only one goal: to liberate the mentally ill. And for this, it is necessary to understand them. You must become conscious of the fact that the healthy and the mentally ill do not stand face to face like man and monster. This must be understood! And so the liberation of the mental patient is not a matter of humanism, but one of understanding.

We must speak of the forces that run deep within the soul, and above all of sexuality, and its deep connections to the personality, and to spiritual attributes and capabilities.

The great battle between the sexual instincts and the ego instincts (or cultural expectations, if preferred) takes place in the dark and is beyond suspicion. Those on the outside have no inclination of what grand warring armies stand face to face in the life of a child.

We cannot see the battle because the soul of a child is a 'tabula rasa'. Yet behind this tabula rasa lies hidden a sexuality in development.

People do not wish to recognise the developing sexuality and sexual curiosity of the child. Adults, in their fear of disturbing their own repressed and forgotten pasts, turn their backs on the child's conspicuous expressions of sexuality. If they fail to notice these, they consider them to be unnatural, sinful, harmful and pernicious.

Yes, there are those weighed down by heredity. But let us not forget that many people do not carry with them a burden passed down by their ancestors, but one acquired from a conflict in childhood. At that time, it was the excessively high barrier of the early years of life, or a barrier that was raised suddenly rather than gradually, that chased back the sexual instincts. This results in the onset of subsidence in the foundations of the soul. If no developmental disturbance appears immediately or for a prolonged period, it lies latent and unnoticed in the individual, like the forgotten sediment on the bed of a river. If life later raises new and greater barricades, the upswell of love is incapable of rising above the new barrier.

Such faults large and small occur in the life of every child, and sediments of this nature can flare up and prompt the flow to be reversed. This is perhaps why most people fear life's new barriers and new trials. Maybe this is why the fear of mental illness lies dormant in so many.

Yes: the healthy and the mentally ill are connected by the desire to return. The healthy and the mentally ill are divided by the sediment, the injury that lies dormant in the patient and was suffered in childhood as a result of the blind brutality of life, rather than always resulting from weakness at birth.

There is no separating wall between the healthy of mind and the mentally ill that the fearful individual feels compelled to raise at any cost. No, my friend, the pitfalls cannot be avoided through the falsification of facts. Instead, let's look at the patient: *he was injured just as most of us were.* And then our primary goal will not be to refuse to comprehend the words of the insane, and instead to lock them away.

There is something the lunatic is trying to say! And then we will perhaps look at his life and culture to see if there might be something to cure.

How can life harm the fresh buds of human existence?

And so I will introduce you to one such poor individual who was wounded early in life.

Caesar Cadavi

For many years, we no longer noticed him at all. Like a long-since meaningless memorial post on the corner of a busy road, he has turned to stone on the spot. He turned to the sky like a sun worshipper. His forehead shone far and wide. His closed eyelids swelled brightly. Shut tight, his mouth arced thinly to his protruding ears. His two bony hands stiffened upwards, inseparably interlocked in prayer.

Cadavi stared at the sky meaninglessly yet with a secret significance. He named himself Caesar when he was admitted to the asylum decades ago. Over the past 15 years, barely any entries had been made in his medical file. It was as if the doctors, of whom so many had fallen by the wayside, had grown tired of making notes about him.

"He stands motionless in a corner. He closes his eyes, he does not talk. He prays silently. His senses have been dulled."

For another month, no more than:

"Status idem."[63]

In Yellow House phraseology, Cadavi's was a case closed.

In the meantime, I spent much time leafing through old medical files. How many times, my friend, have I presided over these faded documents on quiet afternoons in the whitewashed doctors' office? While the aroma of the Hárshegy (lime hill) drifted in, and now and again a yell from a patient or the whistle of a thrush could be heard, how many times did your Telemach take flight into realms so short on boldness?...

In the cupboards, there lay dust-covered fascicles here and there. All thick bundles of documents: "...men released in 1869." "...women released in 1869." "...men deceased in 1869." "... women deceased in 1869," etc. Writings bearing witness to people who lived here for decades and who also died here. Thirty-thousand people: now thirty-thousand sheaves of paper. Fantastically futile struggles in the purple-misty valleys of prehistoric times. I was driven by an irresistible urge to penetrate the soul of Cadavi. Every afternoon at precisely three, the nurse was instructed to bring him into my doctor's office. I kept him there for an hour. He stood there motionless. His eyes were permanently closed. He could not even be seated by force. His head was turned towards the sky.

I sensed that my success would hinge on my perseverance. I made preparations. As I attempted to converse with him, I went about my daily work.

"Sit down, Mr Cadavi!"

Then I continued to write. I later repeated the question.

"Are you not exhausted yet?"

I hazarded countless questions. I tried to approach him from countless angles. Cadavi remained motionless.

I thought my every effort would be in vain when I once asked him on a whim:

"Who are you praying to?"

He jolted as if struck by lightning.

"Who are you praying to?" I asked anew, without knowing myself if I was doing the right thing.

He slumped back as if I had punched him. He turned pale. His eyelids began to tremor. A tear suddenly bubbled out onto his reddish lashes.

A terrifying moment!... Is it right for me

to continue to question him? Would I not set in motion an avalanche of suffering in a patient who has now found calm?

And yet I instinctively had to go on. I was looking for a word... a soothing word:

"Look, Cadavi... don't be afraid... I only want the best for you... be brave!... Speak! Perhaps you are praying to a saint? ...to Maria?"

•

I could not stop. His ten fingers leapt apart. His face became tearful.

And suddenly he opened his eyes up to me.

Two eyes. Two frightened animals... two rudely awakened, tired black dogs baying at me.

I could not stand those eyes boring into me. I took hold of his bony fingers:

"I don't want to hurt you!... Dear Cadavi..."

Cadavi was panting. His fixed gaze broke down, weary. His eyelashes slowly closed.

I was shocked. I carefully interlocked his fingers again, as they do with the dead.

I felt like a mischievous child who had almost spoiled a game. I did not want to hurt him further. I gave up on ever penetrating the soul of Cadavi.

This was, however, not the last of this matter. Cadavi was waiting for them to collect him the following day. At three o'clock, he began fidgeting restlessly.

"Bring him in!" I said enthusiastically. At this, he practically fell into the nurse's arms. Now Cadavi wanted to come...

I steered well clear of the question to finally arrive at it: What does Maria mean to you?

•

One year later, Cadavi started talking. I slowly reached the hidden sediment.

Cadavi once said:

"Something happened seven thousand years ago."

On another occasion, after a long time:

"My life turned around when I was aged five. I need to go back."

Cadavi's declaration did not surprise me. I often heard similar from patients. I need to go back! But what happened seven thousand years ago, at the age of five?

Cadavi spoke of himself in the third person. He was the Little Lad. Maybe he really was known by this nickname. He said Little Lad was a quiet child. He never played. Then he added quietly: "Not always. I think this change came at the age of five."

Little Lad must have been an exemplary child who no one ever saw laugh; who leaves when a guest enters the room. Who makes no demands. There is no way of knowing what he is thinking. One who is waiting for something, but it is impossible to know what.

Perhaps it is precisely this buried experience in which he immerses himself.

Memories rose up:

"Glass-covered corridor. A red leander... Ugly woman. Holds Little Lad. Laughs at Little Lad... Mother ties her corset to make her beautiful and thin... Little Lad likes her, she smells good... Yes... the ugly woman?! She came from the emperor's harem... she wants to kiss Little Lad... Little Lad hits her. The ugly woman stops but carries on laughing. Little Lad's father has an ugly beard... He is the emperor of the harem... Little Lad also hits the emperor of the harem. He also dies, but he too continues to laugh....

"Travel... Yellow, green, red carriages... Little Lad in his mother's lap... thumb-sized people in the valley, little carriages, little haystacks. Little Lad calls out: Tiny horses, little cows, come into my lap... Mother laughs... She says: they are not small, just far away... But dwarves do exist... Yes, is that father? Yes!... Once he beat mother...

"...On the train, Little Lad needs to wee-wee, so mother holds him out of the window. It was very good for Little Lad to be able to wee-wee into the great valley in front of his mother. Little Lad just realised that he is the real Caesar.

"...Yes, father?... Father once locked the door... a large white door. He yells at mother... he throws his hat to the ground... Little Lad is sitting on the floor, frightened, he looks at the broken hat... Little Lad strikes the hat, father has disappeared...

"...A village... Little Lad's mother is lying in the grass... Little Lad runs over... He laughs... Mother does not turn towards him. Little Lad turns her head towards him with force... Mother cries... The cows and mother smell good. Little Lad sleeps with mother... Mother cries. Little Lad strokes her... Mother kisses Little Lad.

"...Father is never coming back, says mother. Little Lad is very happy. Father has died, says Little Lad. No! He's just not coming back. Yes, father? Then he has died. Little Lad is always in mother's bed. Every night for two years. This is how Little Lad remained Caesar.

"...Little Lad is happy by mother's side, he can always feel mother's scent... Little Lad already knows all the months... September... Mother says: Father went away two years ago... Yes? Father died... Little Lad is Caesar.

"...Mother is sitting out on the porch... Little Lad is in bed. He is waiting for mother. Why isn't mother coming? For it is so good when she is here. Every night, the wall opens... dwarf people, horses and tiny cows between mountains... They go through golden gates to a golden palace... Little Lad is Caesar and mother is the empress... It is a very long time before mother comes... he cries out a hundred times: Mother, sweet mother, come already!

"...Yes, what is happening?! Screaming! Ugly harem screaming! Mother rushes in with the emperor of the harem on her arm.

"Father is here, father is here!

"They both kiss Little Lad. Little Lad hits father... Father dies, but carries on laughing. Father takes Little Lad in his lap, strokes him and shows him a picture book...

"Little Lad watches mother make a bed on the divan. This is when Little Lad sees that his mother has betrayed him, she is also of the harem. Little Lad must leave mother's bed."

This is what happened seven thousand years ago, when Little Lad was five years old. He doesn't remember any more. It was into this night that Cadavi's future sank. This was the betrayal Cadavi never recovered from. He repressed and forgot his love's tragedy and went on his way... No one could have suspected that Little Lad was bound to his mother by an eternal love-hate relationship. For a long time, there was no visible sign of this blockage. Cadavi repressed and forgot that night. Instead, he became withdrawn into himself, afraid of the night and of noises. His anxious dreams brought wrestling bouts and earth tremors...

And life passed by without him ever feeling love.

He completed his studies with distinction. Then he travelled abroad to continue his research into history. He met a girl in Berlin. She too was a historian. A deep friendship developed between the two young doves.

And Cadavi wanted to love, but he was unable. Cadavi was swept into the fate that lay in wait for him by a desire for love without the capacity to love.

The poor boy only had desires, which were good for nothing more than to shake the bond to his mother and with it his old disappointment, despair and hate... everything that he buried within himself on that fateful night. Unfathomable hatred stirred within the young man. Anger with nowhere to go!

Anger with nowhere to go! Stimulated by the experiences of an evening long forgotten, it is the emotions associated with these that bubble up into consciousness. Terrible, tortuous, incomprehensible, and unresolvable emotions!

Anger with nowhere to go!

Cadavi went into a rage one night in his flat, repeatedly stabbing his girlfriend. They took him to the lunatic asylum.

This is all Cadavi says about that night:

"She had blue eyes, blond hair and was called Maria." She was Little Lad's mother, the empress of the harem, in disguise.

Yes, my friend, that is it: she had blue eyes, blond hair and was called Maria!

Cadavi's mother really was called Maria. I am entirely sure she was blond-haired and blue-eyed. This must have been a decisive factor even when the young man began to take an interest in a blond girl with blue eyes in the library in Berlin.

In the Yellow House, as it is said, the religious madness broke out in Cadavi.

The boy, aged five, was struck down by a sudden sense of betrayal in his love for his mother and was, as a result, never able to truly break free of her. He fled his mother into a life without love because love would only have led him back to his mother with all its might. And Cadavi went, went and went until he fell into the arms of a Maria with blue eyes and blond hair.

When, on that fateful Berlin night, he recognised his mother in this girl in his delirium, he once again fled – from reality – into mental illness. He had to become mentally ill so he would never again encounter Maria, real or in disguise.

But in vain!

Cadavi began to pray. The mechanical whispering of the prayers grew quieter, and the poor patient, fixated on the sky, now became inseparably united with a heavenly empress – who is known as Maria and who is doubtless blond-haired and blue-eyed.

Ghosts that Return Home

Do you remember that, when I told this story, one of you remarked:

"En revient toujours..."[64]

Yes, the love I so violently drive away returns to me. Anger driven away and smothered indicates a soul poorly tended to. Successful surrender demands work. It is better to examine the pain, to confront it openly, if we want to be done with it forever. But the child is not strong enough to face such early, unexpected and inexplicable traumas, and can do no more than to suffocate and forget a pain that is intolerably tortuous.

And most of the repression is manifested by the child in its sexuality. The battle of the sex instincts with the ego instincts. We might also say that it is the struggle between sexuality and culture.

Yet this is also the path of personal development.

The first object of a boy's love is his mother. However, this love clashes with a cultural taboo: he cannot love his mother in the romantic sense, only in the form of tender affection. This is the inexorable ancient Oedipus complex upon which all of our loving swell breaks with a greater or lesser degree of trauma, and which decided the fate of man and mankind.

When the boy's incestuous love becomes separated from the mother, it breaks into countless forms of love as he constructs a transfigured, inaccessible image of the mother in place of the object of his love. As such, the example and warning of the ideal elevated in place of the love object will lead the boy throughout his life, taking him from instinctive desires to intellectual goals and connecting him to a thousand 'sublimated' love objects. It is into these Ego-ideals that alongside the parents, teachers, educators, outstanding individuals, the heroes of history, and cultural combatants, are then gathered...

The Ego-ideal is formed from the first love, the denial of the incestuous love. It is under its guidance that the ego instincts create the Ego itself from the sexual instincts. Sexuality is the raw material from which the ego instinct, the sculptor, models the Ego. The force that thinks and stands guard at the gates of action.

This is how our culture came about.

The first cultural activity was the creation of fire, which was originally a symbolic sexual act. Sexual intercourse, prohibited for particular reasons, was playfully imitated through the rubbing together of two pieces of wood. The act permitted in this form led man to the method of kindling fire.

A game that had in this way become of cultural utility grew even more desexualised. Culture is therefore essentially the expression of desexualised love instincts.

Culture is driven by the same amorous outpouring that has been forced up by the constraints on the ego instincts.

Any individual can constrain their sexuality only to a certain extent in allowing them to be useful to their culture and preventing them from being harmful to themselves.

If the constraint is too great, the repressed sexuality – the ghost – may return in the form of neuroses and psychoses.

Mental illness springs from the unequal struggle between the sexual instincts and culture, when the Ego-ideals demand excessive repression of sexuality, and with it stultify the will directed towards the outside world.

My friend, when people openly and furtively mock and pity the poor lunatic, I am repeatedly reminded of their fatal short-sightedness. Because the poor lunatic serves as an unwilling and unwitting *martyr protesting against the culture.* We are afraid of the lunatic, we smile at him and pity him, but we fail to see the culture that may in actual fact be the tragedy we all suffer.

•

And we don't see the tragedy in the child.

Despite the best efforts of those raising the child: they will only reach the child when they recognise that the sexual question raises an insurmountable wall between the child and the adult.

The poor, radiant child – my friend – stands by this wall incredibly neglected. The grown-ups don't want to and don't know how to understand the little ones because they have denied, and perhaps repressed and forgotten, the sexuality of their own childhood, but certainly condemned it...

The child's bodily impulses rap ever more forcefully. Boys and girls all stand confused before exhilarating and terrifying wonders... Uncomprehending, they endure and enjoy the desires that strain their bodies and their souls...

The instinctive desires for love are set against the taboos of the Ego-ideal. When lust bursts in with force, fears and concerns rise up. The battle between the desires and the Ego-ideal of the child can only be fought by the child herself. This is one of life's most weighty tasks.

The child does not dare ask. She very quickly learns what things she is not permitted to inquire about. The child notices that all adults stand in opposition to her and lie to her. Her whole thinking and behaviour turns away like an inverted heliotropic flower. She senses where the thing the society of adults is keeping secret begins. Yet this secrecy also reveals how little they know about the astonishingly high level of the child's intellect and instinctive intuition. This naivety arouses the suspicion that adults unconsciously do indeed do everything they can to reveal the secret. The child always senses when talk turns to *that thing* once again... She sees how they suddenly fall silent in anticipation, how they speak a foreign language, how they smile at one another, how they are punished over an insignificant matter. She senses that all this is obvious, some kind of smile or a form of sign language about the same secret. All this evidence is augmented by the street, which is not so cautious, the shop windows, as well as schoolmates and servants, who are more honest, and the books stuffed beneath the school desk...

But the child creates its Ego-ideal all the while. She accepts all the lies the adults tell her. In this phase of her development, the child represses and forgets, already entering the society of adults as someone who has learned the privilege of adults: lies and deceit.

And, my friend, there is plenty more we need to talk about!

Every adult condemns masturbation because he has been informed that it is a sin and a serious danger to health that the child must be protected from. Sometimes, however, the adult pursues the child with fire and brimstone and considers this the most important aspect of his task in nurturing the child. But this is often none other than the disturbed and poorly repressed onanism complex of the parents. Desire once repressed rears its head in the form of the spectre of masturbation and the persecution of masturbation.

Intimidation does not generally bring success. This is because the intimidation always conceals some form of exaggeration and deceit. The child perceives himself as an outcast from society, the only one who commits the acts in question.

A child may improve in response to intimidation. But desire is often more powerful than the will of the child. Thus every lapse breaks off a piece from the young person's self-confidence. The unintended outcome of intimidation is therefore a severe sense of *guilt.*

Feelings of worthlessness, shame, uncertainty and cowardice all stem from this sense of guilt. The child blushes, becomes confused and forgetful: *all those symptoms erroneously attributed to masturbation – are caused by deceit.*

Yes, the blushing, confused, cowardly, listless and forgetful young man was most often made so not by masturbation, but by a sense of guilt. The lie he has been inoculated with: "You are the world's most worthless person."

•

The struggle of the child plays out between his primal sexual desire and his cultural self. This is one of life's most onerous challenges. This coming-together can be of the same elemental force and laden with such betrayal that, as with Cadavi, the child is unable to cope and has no choice but to repress it on account of its intolerable shamefulness. *This he achieves and then, without him actually being conscious of it, the conflict remains fixated to his capacity to love only on a primeval level.*

On the primeval level?! Yes! Our entire instinctive past consists of incomprehensible primitive instinct fragments that mankind perhaps brought with him from primordial life forms. These are the primitive types of eroticism, such as oral, anal, muscular and so on, as well as sadism, bisexuality, homosexuality, and others. A whole host of *antisocial instincts* rumble through the soul of the child... Components of eroticism that are now all in stark opposition to the natural, as well as the social and cultural, environment.

How does the child cope with these desires, what happens to the remains of these wild prehistoric animals that cannot be lived out?

One part of them dissolves into the development process. This state of amalgamation is what results in normal sexuality. Normality is the optimal blend of countless instinct fragments, much as white light is a coming-together of the seven colours. So the unification of childhood perversions under genitality is what produces normality.

Another group of the part-instincts disappears in the same way the Oedipus complex disappeared, when affection for the mother became tender love and the love of higher ideals. The part-instincts dissolve into the character through sublimation. From anal eroticism, the naïve delight in beauty contrasted with the child's bodily needs, are sublimated cleanliness, order, frugality and ambition.

Some sexual desires, on the other hand, are satisfied directly by sexual means. Any individual is only able to constrain his or her sexual desire *to a certain extent* without this becoming harmful. Excessive repression produces neurotic symptoms. These symptoms are regularly observed as fear, compulsive behaviour and guilt. But in these, the forbidden desire itself, albeit in contorted form, is also satisfied. The ghost returns.

Eventually, the repressed desire and the primitive part-instinct – such as sadism – may surge forth with all their brutality. These appear as outbreaks of untrammelled anger that simultaneously assault the apparently calm soul. Unfathomable and horrific acts that bear witness to the immeasurable power of unconscious instincts and the constraints of conscious forces.

Returning ghosts!

Life and Death

Let us forget, my friend, everything I have said about the sexual instinct and the ego instinct, so that we can better understand an even more comprehensive phenomenon: the life and death drives.

I have had the moment of death described to me more than once. One person told me how his experience of being deathly ill and feverishly delirious felt like tossing and turning on a stormy sea. The waves threatened to sweep him off deck at any moment. He felt the only way to escape death was to hold fast to the ropes of the mast.

But a sailor with the look of a pirate kept pulling him away. After a struggle that seemed to last an eternity, he was just about able to cling to the rope and survive.

I myself was once ill with a fever when I was a child. I didn't understand what was happening to me. It felt as if my body had melted into exhilarating velvet. Every fibre of the velvet prickled and vibrated. This was interrupted by an enormous bang. It was frightening, but it was rushing to my aid. This banging sound returned over and over, assisting me countless times, shaking all that vibrating velvet to dust. Suddenly, however, I found myself alone. The bang didn't come. I became deathly stiff. Everything inside me slowly turned over. This cartwheel – I felt – was the end of me. Now I was dying.

Eventually, there struck from somewhere, with the enthusiasm of a latecomer, the miraculous brass rod. That's when I tore something off. It was the compress on my neck. I coughed and my throat cleared. The tremors ceased. The brass rod now returned thick and fast and fell quiet. I recognised it as the ticking of our pendulum clock.

•

As death approaches, two pedlars haggle over something: the death drive, intent on returning the ejected material to the inorganic world, and the life drive, which strives to keep it alive through contact with the outside world.

This is similar to the struggle between returning to magical omnipotence, to the primeval calm and the womb of the earth, and clinging to reality.

The life drive grabs hold, and the death drive denies the ticking that binds to life those called to live it.

It wasn't the ticking of the pendulum clock that saved my life. And yet, in the delirium of approaching death, it nevertheless took on a deep, symbolic significance.

In any case, the pendulum clock, as a human creation, was projected by man from his own being. Perhaps a great secret of his being is expressed in it. So perhaps from the very machinery of our existence – the life and death drives – man projects part of a secret onto this mechanism for measuring time, the pendulum clock.

The Pendulum Clock

The hefty weight that desires to return to the centre of the earth symbolises the death drive... Left to itself, it would plummet downwards at insane speed... Ephemeral life would turn to immediate death.

But the suspended weight cannot fall freely. The cord supporting the weight is wound around the shaft of a gear wheel. This is prevented from twisting back by the anchor, which moves back and forth, clinging to the gear. Driven by the swinging of the pendulum, this anchor always both releases the weight to descend by one degree at a time, while also holding it back by one degree.

The pendulum, the life drive, does not allow the weight, the death drive, to fall. Both together thus maintain a certain tension: life.

A tiny audibly ticking bottleneck moving the hands of the clock forward: Life. A silent and slow little fall of the weight downwards: Death.

Taking place amid this tension between the life and death drives is the act of living itself, just as what we call social *love* arises from the tension between the sexual – love – instincts and the Ego – hate – instincts.

A life filled with the desire for love swings like a pendulum across the dead centre through the tension between the life and death drives.

The clock itself symbolises the union of Eros, divided into man and woman, and the beginning of life.

Do you people feel that when you become gods at the highest level of the love arc, when the powerful pendulum swinging into the void reaches its zenith in agony and lust, do you feel, people, as mortals returning to the inorganic world, that – for a moment – you have passed through the dead centre?!

In the embrace of love, when life is springing forth from you, do you not feel that something inside of you is dying?

Death

I have one last little story to add here.

There was an 85-year-old gentleman named Mr Csetényi who was at one time an 'honorary' resident of the Yellow House. He was brought there because he had no one and could not survive in the outside world. His admission papers stated that he suffered from dementia. The old man was happy to be able to lie down in a clean bed, and he no longer had any troubles in life.

One day, it was reported that the elderly gentleman had a pocket knife, which he tended to forget in his bedroom. On my rounds, I said to him:

"Mr Csetényi, you know that you are free to do as you wish here. But please, take better care of your pocket knife as some of the patients in the room where you sleep are not trustworthy."

Mr Csetényi promised not to forget the little knife when he left the bedroom, but soon enough we found ourselves having to bring it to him again.

So I told him to choose another dorm, whichever one he liked, where the knife wouldn't pose a threat.

"Doctor, no. Not for all the world. I beg of you, let me stay!"

"Well then, please hand over the knife every evening. Either to me or to someone else. It will be returned in the morning."

"Doctor, no! I would never give up my little knife for all the world," pleaded the old man with tears in his eyes. "I beg of you, let me keep it."

And so it went on for a while, until finally it was no longer possible to leave it at that. One day, I asked him politely, "Mr Csetényi, please give me the pocket knife. I'll keep it overnight, and you'll get it back in the morning."

The good old fellow pleaded, but I remained adamant. He slowly took the knife out of his waistcoat pocket, handed it over with a shaking hand and said despairingly:

"Doctor, if you take away my penicillin, I will die."

The old man's sorrow was painful to witness. There was no way I could console him. Hurt, he turned away and shuffled off.

Mr Csetényi went to bed, came down with a fever that night and contracted pneumonia the next day. He never spoke another word. A few days later, he was dead.

That's how he died. Perhaps it was my fault, because I didn't understand what the pocketknife meant to the old man. Or perhaps it was how you wanted it, Mr Csetényi.

War and Peace

The disintegration of the harmony between the life and death drives, between hatred and love...

After wars and revolutions, people are gripped by a particular interest in knowing how these events affect mental patients.

Unfortunately, I was also unable to satisfy the reporters' curiosity in this regard. The experience offers nothing remarkable, and the question doesn't even interest me. I am more interested in the opposite question:

How did the mentally ill influence wars and revolutions?

What I mean by my question is this: how did the lunatic, who emerged wounded from his battle with culture, come to influence war, revolution and history?

•

It is often said, my friend, that mental illness and war are somehow related. Mental illness is the state of war within certain individuals, while war is the mental illness of the masses. It is certain that both unfold in the spirit of return, of the death drive, of destruction.

War also arises from the breakdown of the life and death drives, which I might also say was the disintegration of the harmony between love and hate.

What we call social love is actually not a drive, but a set of component instincts. The hate impulses of the death drive and the love impulses of the life drive reach equilibrium in their opposing tension (as I attempted to explain with the example of the pendulum clock), and this dual drive acting together *is love*. Love is not a unified feeling. In the machinery of the soul, opposing drives are constantly clashing, and this dynamic ideally maintains a balance. In love, we only see the side of this balancing act that we wish to see. But even if the hate impulses do not come to the surface, we must never forget they exist and that they may one day become active.

It is enough to simply observe children without prejudice. Like members of primitive societies, they express their hatred much more than we do. If the strictures of their upbringing do not hinder them too strongly, their hatred becomes sadistic, and even their death wishes are frequently expressed to their beloved parents.

This is clearly confirmed by the primitive folk custom of killing and devouring the father. Eating the father, in addition to satisfying the most ancient component instinct, that of oral eroticism, was also accompanied by the belief that the son would absorb all of his father's strength and virtue. The devouring of the predecessor is thus also the basic form of the development of the Ego-ideal. Yes, my friend, this is how the most horrible things can become sublime. Because, with the subsequent development of culture, instead of the father, it was only the symbol of the father, the totem, the sacred animal of the tribe, that would be consumed. With even further sublimation and binding of the original hateful feelings, all that remains today is the desire for the offspring to inherit all the virtues of the father. Thus, with the development of the Ego-ideal, the act of *physically* eating the father was replaced by that of doing so *figuratively*.

In this way, forbidden hateful emotions can be guided by the Ego ideal towards higher purposes that are permitted by society. This process, sublimation, is a more successful way of dealing with our antisocial instincts than crudely repressing them. We see such sublimated sadism in the many games and competitions engaged in by both children and adults, in hunting, in sport, and in certain professional occupations, the medical profession, in surgery, and so on.

War, on the other hand, is not the sublimation of instincts, as some have claimed in its justification. War is the crude eruption of poorly repressed sadism.

As I said, sadism can be repressed. When repressed, the drives are unable to emerge in any way. Drives, however, operate on the unconscious level, cause tension, and eventually erupt in raw and undisguised fashion, or rise to the surface in various perverse forms and circuitous ways. There are those who defend themselves against their antisocial instincts, such as the urge to commit murder, by drowning out their intolerable impulses with loving desires.

We are no strangers to this type of neurotic.

These are the same individuals who tremble when an insect is crushed. They are the gardeners left with the unsolved problem of whether to cultivate fruit or caterpillars.

Thus, there are neurotics who torture themselves for this same reason and out of a sense of guilt. Very often, they attempt to defend themselves against the intrusion of their hateful desires with acts of excessive benevolence and fervent love for others.

My friend, sometimes people who feel the need to proclaim from the rooftops that they are willing to die or kill for their principles occupy my thoughts. Through an ideology, they conceal the unpleasant inner reality from their consciences. What motivates them on the unconscious level: the urge to kill.

Hatred leads them to the ideal.

There are revolutionaries who wish to kill monarchs for the sake of an ideal. They have no inkling that a wonderful ideology needed to be constructed within them because they are locked in an eternal battle with the father. They mishandled their Oedipus complexes.

And hatred dressed in the shining armour of an ideology is a fatal one!

Although such individuals might at first

find it heartening to feel themselves superior to others *with their most sacredly held virtues, family, religion, race, the nation or humanity as a whole, they very often, albeit unconsciously, find a way to express their poorly repressed sadism and confer upon themselves the license to murder and destroy without remorse.*

•

War and revolution, though, indicate the return of poorly repressed sadism. No matter how brutal it sounds and no matter how much it offends human dignity, I must say, my friend, that all of us contribute to war. War is made by everyone, and is made within everyone. All the bestiality and vandalism to be manifested in war must be unconsciously repressed somewhere in the soul, waiting for the day of its resurrection. Preparations for war are being made without pause. Those preparing with the greatest urgency are those *pushing for it* and those *fighting against it*. Those who preach peace and love and those who manufacture weapons are both preparing for war: one unconsciously, the other consciously.

From our culture and its fullest accomplishments emerges a poorly repressed sadism.

Our culture is described as technological. Rightly so!

Machines are conceived in the name of making our lives happier and distributing the wealth of the earth among as many people as possible.

But lurking behind this pretence are hatred and greed...

A machine is an extension of man's muscles. However, the muscles were originally created for struggle and to enable us to satisfy our hatred and desire to kill. Machines designed for happiness now clearly demonstrate the return of this poorly repressed role of our muscles.

Yes, my dear friend: *giant machines, terrible explosives and murderous gases will serve a humanity weary of this culture against millions of their brethren, just as Cain's brawny fist served him, albeit solely against his one brother.*

•

Peace is not a question of love. *Peace can only be achieved through an understanding of the unconscious forces of our souls.*

Those who yearn for peace should not speak of love until they have known hatred. As with all other indestructible and thus necessary resources, the hate impulses must be reckoned with coldly.

The technical advances of our century have realised an age-old dream of mankind. We are now able to fly through the sky in machines heavier than air. And this was only made possible by taking account of the force of the earth's gravity. Man realised that the force of gravity – the weight of air and its capacity to generate lift – was absolutely necessary for flight.

Like flight, so is peace: *an attainable dream.*

But the engineers of peace must reckon with the law of the gravity of the human soul; to reckon with a mother earth from which all forces emanate and whose eternal draw will, on account of the tension of opposing forces, one day give us the gift of flight...

...The same mother earth to which we must *carefully* descend from time to time!

Those who long for *eternal* flight entirely detached from the ground will eventually be yanked back to it by mother earth's eternal force, they will not be anchored on earth – they must inexorably come crashing down!

This we are taught by Heroes, Poets and Fools.

Cities – Mothers

Cities are built as is the way of the world, and cities are destroyed. But emerging in advance of the destruction are ideological wars: over materialism, idealism, nationalism, capitalism, proletarianism and, most recently, fascism and Bolshevism – a rich arsenal of notions. But let us not imagine that the notion is of significance in war. No, as soon as there is no longer a delusion or hallucination at the heart of the matter, but an inadequately repressed primal urge that finally breaks forth, the walls of the city come tumbling down.

War arises from the same psychological need the two enemies share. Every war is a war against culture. Against the city.

And the city is a symbol of the mother.

The tragedy of humanity is therefore the tragedy of Caesar Cadavi. He is separated from his mother, and by repressing his love for her and erecting his Ego-ideal, he creates culture and builds cities. Then he finds that the notion, the city, represses the primal urges too much. So the city must be destroyed, because the city is also a mother.

Humanity must destroy and build cities many more times before it can create a world in which primary drives are not repressed, but are instead sublimated, and the demands of culture converge in harmony without damaging either the individual or society.

My friend! None of God's fruits ripen later than man!

A Fantasy

Before I tell you what a mental patient is, I'd like to share with you a flight of fancy.

How could it have happened?

In the beginning, the earth was without

form or shape... And even as God was creating out of the dust his greatest triumph, man, he was contemplating how he could protect him from ever learning the secret of that creation. Because all God intended to create was man, not an omniscient being. But this proved no trifling matter, for does the secret of creation not reside inside the living creation itself, just as the secret of the clock resides in its mechanism? Would man not merely have to look within to see how, out of dust, he came to be?

God's wisdom is infinite. He did not deny people their inward-looking spiritual vision, but he did give them physical eyes, so the great brightness that is outside in the world would prevent them from gazing inward.

Man has been looking outwards ever since: digging up the earth, drilling, carving, building and destroying. And he cannot rest, for he is searching outside for something he will never find: the secret to his Ego, to his own self.

But even so!

Everything he sees in the world is nothing but himself; everything he shaped in the world and anything he ever thought about the world was no different: merely his own self.

He modelled his first weapons and tools on his fists, arms, fingernails, and teeth. Later, he projected not only his muscles onto primitive machines, but also the chemical processes in his laboratory, which were later found to take place in the stomach, intestines, kidneys and glands. Today, it is clearly evident that humanity's great inventions, resources and instruments measuring the infinite are projected copies of the human nervous system, senses and cognitive mechanisms.

While God was forcing man to turn to the outside world, man unconsciously looked inward and etched his eyes, heart and nervous system into his culture.

•

But there is one man who has completely turned away from the world, who has no need for all your brilliance: the despised lunatic, who instead gazes into the terrifying past, where he sees – perhaps through the ancient lineage of mothers – the miracle: the secret law of creation.

What is a Lunatic?

Soldiers marching down endless highways: people reduced to rags.

There are three types of subversive among them:

Some merely pretend to march but gradually fall behind. These are the 'go-slow' strikers:[65] the neurotics... And the poets.

There are those who secretly rip up the railway tracks and throw bombs into your midst. These are the saboteurs: the antisocial types... And the heroes.

And then there are those who simply break rank:

"I will not go along with you."

These are the open strikers: the mentally ill.

They, the screamers and the silenced, the praying and the cursing, the humiliated and the exalted: it is as if they are speaking in the never-understood language of the prophets to the wearily advancing masses:

"Look over here! In our wounds pulses the law of all our blood that has been violated. Our love broke upon your cities – upon our mothers – and we destroy your unloving walls with hatred. We are the sick, but it is you healthy people who must be healed! Through us, the dreaming heroes, storytellers and lunatics, the axis of history creaks towards new, incredible cities and possibilities for life."

3

The Redemption Of The Lunatics — The Liberation Of The Sane

What more remains?

I am in debt to the throngs of people who have stood at the doors of the Yellow House for years, anxiously waiting with their little purses... Those who struggle in the trap hoping to somehow sneak out.

"In God's name, let me out, I am innocently locked up!"

Never has a complaint been so poorly understood.

We Telemachs adroitly explain that they are not locked up. This is not a prison. And they have not been convicted.

But they were standing before the court of humanity. It was not the sentence, the Yellow House, that was the most severe punishment, but the label:

"Poor lunatic!"

•

How many times I have told myself, "I don't know how it could ever be good, but the way it is now is truly awful."

Just look at the predecessors of the Yellow House: there was a time when the workhouse and the poorhouse, lepers and victims of scurvy, the plague and syphilis, fallen women, orphans and the aged, and the homes of the executioner and the dog catcher could all be found lined up outside the city walls, together with the madhouse. Then they built towers, and later buildings akin to barracks and monasteries, and later still pavilions, and eventually more modern and humane sanatoriums. Everywhere, however, there remained the bars, the stone walls, the cells, and, as the most important implement in the hand of the doctor: the key.

My friend! This is the original sin of the Yellow House!

Mental institution, sanatorium! It still has something of the prison about it. The doctor is still also a jailer, whose superhuman task it is to make the occupants forget they are in prison.

"I was brought here by force, and am being kept here by force, Doctor, I protest..."

"It is not by force, just in your own interest... you must rest... be patient!"

To another, we say he has not been permanently admitted. He's simply under observation.

Be patient! Then we must wait to hear the verdict of the court. And then, the court is yet to decide. Be patient!

After that, be patient, because a permanent guardian is yet to be assigned, then we do not yet have consent from your family for your release. And then, the council hasn't signed the form. Then, I consented, but he did not. Then, he consents, but I do not. Be patient!

And while the patient is subjected to this humiliating game of pass the buck, weeks go by, then months and years, as they are wrapped in a mendacious web of *impersonal* authority that cannot be held to account.

And in the end?

One starts to yell, rip off his clothes, smash the window and rattle the bars.

Then the report is made: The patient is in a rage!

It is not only the mental patient who is raging, but also the confined, humiliated and desperate human being.

Another will pull his blankets over his head and bid farewell to the world.

The report: The patient has fallen into a stupor!

No! Confined, humiliated and desperate, he has fled into oblivion.

•

The Yellow House is the rich soil – that sought by the sick person in withdrawal – of an unreal world.

Any number of 'cavemen' kept in a cell for decades have been lured into the sunlight and roused into a more human way of life with regular stimulation! But the monotony of the Yellow House buries all that revivifies once more.

When I saw the contorted souls the Yellow House had frozen solid – my friend – there arose in me grave concerns about our humanism.

They gathered up the village idiots. They locked them up among the many sick. Why? Because they are afraid of them. But faced with the legitimate protection of the public, the legitimate interests of the patient were lost. I dare say that the unfortunate lunatic running wild, when teased by children, barked at by dogs, shoved by heartless people, and always bumping against the cruel realities of life, is forced at least to enter into some kind of genuine relationship with life, and maybe even life itself will be of more help than to lie forgotten in a cell in a world alien to his body and soul, only to create a small village with wooden towers for himself in his hallucinations.

Everyone is on the Path of Return

The Yellow House was built for self-defence and comfort. But there is also a primal urge hidden in its creation, one that inspires everyone to return to the primordial mist.

Let there exist in this world burdened with obligations a place where one can live without responsibilities or work. *This terrifying house is at once a house of the heart's desires.* Calvary is at once Nirvana.

If the patient is restless, we calm him with sedatives, kind words, the furnishings of the house, serenity, and baths. The doctor is proud when his ward is quiet and peaceful.

Peace and quiet!

"Be patient! Calm down! Don't shout! Speak softly! Do not tear things up! Do not make a mess! Do not damage the furniture! Do not harass the other patients."

One light-hearted patient of mine once asked:

"Why did I come to your madhouse if I cannot do exactly what I please even here?"

Peace and quiet! As if that were the alpha and omega of psychological healing. We do not concern ourselves with – because we cannot concern ourselves with them – all those kept sickly and silent, hidden under their blankets and immersed in themselves for years on end.

The other reason we create silence and tranquillity is that we strive for silence within ourselves, too. The Yellow House is Nirvana for all of us.

We Telemachs are curing ourselves.

Let us examine the Telemachs!

The Telemachs

How did Telemach become a psychiatrist?

There was never any doubt: he felt a calling. He did, however, question himself once. It made for bitter work – he finally ventured into the analysis of his soul – but the answer emerged.

He remembers a school outing. He was hiking in the hills. Suddenly, the teacher pointed towards the valley:

"That there with the red roof is the madhouse," he said. The boys pushed and shoved each other.

"That's where you belong too. Careful, don't get too close, or they'll put you away!"

Even the teacher laughed! Why are they laughing at the sick?

Telemach's life was already cursed by fear. Where from? My dear friend! This would require me to recount the analysis of a soul, hazy stories... from distant antiquity... about the hail that struck the feeble human seedling, about the sad past that was silently snowed in... However it happened, Telemach, fearing illness himself, secretly became a friend of the ill.

The image of the red-roofed building floated invisibly before him everywhere he went. Slowly but surely, it grew into a compulsion that made his life's path ever narrower. He had to become a doctor. A career had already beckoned. And as he ran from it, the Yellow House suddenly stood before him. That which had been repressed now returned.

A returning ghost!

This is the story of Telemach's calling.

I am afraid that the callings and the Telemachs were all born of sadness...

•

A silvery autumn day. I'm sitting in the park. Piano music from the ward tumbles down beneath the branches. Orbs of sound. This is what one of my patients called the hallucination.

There is something trance-like about sitting here alone as a disturbed girl tinkles out the Barcarole. The auditory procession slowly breaks up. A handful of notes still cascade asunder. Then silence.

Then Telemach set off on his rounds, every afternoon at exactly four o'clock. Empty corridors and rooms. Cool air. Shiny parquet floors. The walls adorned with oil paintings gleam, and the scent wafting in from the gardens mingles with the scent of turpentine, snuff, sourdough bread, iodoform and lavatories. So familiar! This is the sad, triumphant mood of every damp autumn as it returns over the decades. Slowly and silently, the orbs of time flew by, lovely round years, like the orbs of sound... Was this reality, or just another fantasy? It is of no importance: it was painful, beautiful. Telemach was a doctor of the Yellow House. Not of real life.

I have visited many, many lunatic asylums, all manner of similar institutions in distant foreign lands. I was amazed to see everywhere – Telemachs. People withdrawn into themselves. People standing on high. People who understand and forgive everything. Sensitive people. Calm people who are suffering inside. In other words, people who have fled life's stormy sea for the haven of an island. Those who are never cured of the Yellow House: die from it.

One spring day when I was young and in the honeymoon of my career, I took a stroll in the flower garden of the Yellow House with another doctor who was two or three years older than me. I talked about the future. My plans, desires and doubts. My colleague remained silent for a long time. Then, softly, he said:

"Well, is it really worth making plans for those 30 or 40 years?"

The Liberation of the Lunatics

Little by little, I started to realise why it is that the Telemachs are unable to liberate the mentally ill. Yet this is what they constantly strive for. This liberation effort has been under way for over a century. Pinel, the famous psychiatrist of the great French revolutionary period, removed the shackles from the mentally ill, and we have been doing the same ever since.[66] There must clearly be some kind of fault with the liberation, if all we are doing even today is liberating.

Associations were formed to protect the rights of the mentally ill and to assist the cured. Ten years ago, a major movement was launched in America with great determination and a promising outlook. What distinguishes this movement most of all is the fact that its enthusiastic founder and zealous apostle came not from the ranks of the Telemachs, but from among the patients: a cured mental patient named Clifford W. Beers.[67] With quiet admiration, I am observing the tremendous work this man is doing. But they will only achieve success in this worthy endeavour if they can identify the question of our time when it comes to the issue of the mental patient. *This is the question of the healthy people.*

The mentally ill will be liberated only once the healthy are freed from their own tyranny.

The process of liberation has been ongoing for millennia, and all in vain.

Liberation from chains is not the essence of the question, but rather moral liberation from the latent, terrifying stigma: 'lunatic'.

Nevertheless, there is someone who has taken the first decisive step of this act of liberation. Someone who has comprehended the lunatic. His name is already known around the world today, but tomorrow he will herald the reclamation of our souls:

Freud.

He demonstrated that the patient is not insane, that perhaps it is just pretence, and that there is just as much sense in his words as there is in those of healthy people.

With Freud, a new idea was set in motion.

•

This new idea is the Unconscious.

The patient was never understood through his conscious communications. He was out of his mind. It fell upon someone to reveal another realm of the soul that made the Lunatic comprehensible. This other realm: the Unconscious. *The Unconscious became the Archimedean point for the mysteries of the soul.*

The Unconscious.

Despite its familiar name, this remains an unfamiliar concept, much like the Cosmos in days gone by. Freud's Unconscious is not a theoretically conceived concept, but the tangible result of the practical work of studying the soul, of psychoanalysis.

The infinite vastness, depth and inscrutable power of the sea is the only analogy fit to convey a faint sense of the Unconscious. It envelops our egos like the sea envelops a ship; it is the cradle and grave of our egos just as the sea is for the ship, and it is as unfathomable to us as the sea to the ship.

Freud saw gaping in their souls an invisible sea that until now had only be spoken of by the mentally ill in their symbols, and sung by poets in their intuitive whimsy.

Though the ship is on high,
And the ocean surges below,
The water remains the Lord![68]

Sándor Petőfi

•

Freud: one man against the self-love of the world.

Freud tells us that the narcissism of man has been dealt three blows by science. First, when he lost his belief that the earth was at the centre of the universe. This was the *cosmological* trauma. Secondly, when it emerged that he was not a distinct crowning glory of creation, but just another part of the animal kingdom. This was his *biological* trauma. However, the gravest injury came when the sovereignty of his ego was laid bare by psychoanalysis: his *psychological* trauma.

The thinking person is not the master of his own house on account of the intervention of a more powerful domain: the Unconscious. Thus, according to Freud:[69]

"Man feels himself to be supreme within his own mind. Somewhere in the core of his ego, he has developed an organ of observation to keep a watch on his impulses and actions and see whether they harmonize with its demands.

In certain diseases, the ego feels uneasy... Thoughts emerge suddenly without one's knowing where they come from, nor can one do anything to drive them away. These alien guests even seem to be more powerful than those which are at the ego's command. Or else impulses appear which seem like those of a stranger, so that the ego disowns them; yet it has to fear them and take precautions against them...

Psychiatry, it is true, denies that such things mean the intrusion into the mind of evil spirits from without. It can only say with a shrug, 'Degeneracy, hereditary disposition, constitutional inferiority!' Psychoanalysis sets out to explain these uncanny disorders:

Nothing has entered into you from without; a part of the activity of your own mind has been withdrawn from your knowledge and from the command of your will... The blame, I am bound to say, lies with yourself. You overestimated your strength when you thought you could treat your sexual instincts as you liked and could utterly ignore their intentions. The result is that they have rebelled and have taken their own obscure paths to escape this suppression; they have established their rights in a manner you cannot approve. All you have learned is the outcome of their work – the symptom which you experience as suffering. Thus you do not recognise it as a derivative of your own rejected instincts and do not know that it is a substitutive satisfaction of them.

You feel sure that you are informed of all that goes on in your mind if it is of any importance at all, because, in that case, you believe, your consciousness gives you news of it. And if you have had no information of something in your mind, you confidently assume that it does not exist there. Indeed, you go so far as to regard what is 'mental' as identical with what is 'conscious' – that is, with what is known to you in spite of the most obvious evidence that a great deal more must constantly be going on in your mind than can be known to your consciousness. Come, let yourself be taught something on this one point!

What is in your mind does not coincide with what you are conscious of; whether something is going on in your mind and whether you hear of it are two different things. Turn your eyes inward, look into your own depths, learn first to know yourself! Then you will understand why you were bound to fall ill; and perhaps, you will avoid falling ill in future."

And thus psychoanalysis set out to re-educate the ego.

•

The one who had to learn this first was Telemach. The doctor's instrument should be in order after all. His instrument: his own psyche.[70] All humans have gone through the same psychic conflicts that the mental patient is struck down by.

The mentally ill stir up primeval struggles in every person, struggles from which even the doctor instinctively flees.

All of us, doctors included, have psychological blind spots when it comes to mental illness.

The psychiatrist is in a somewhat similar situation to the eye doctor, who must first correct any flaws in his own vision if he wishes to achieve the intended results. Without this correction, the psychiatrist will not understand the phenomena transpiring before his eyes: in fact, he will not even see it. He will be forced to silence, shush and mute the patient at all costs, and his efforts will be directed towards instilling calm. Calm in the House – calm in himself in actual fact.

However, once the doctor has liberated his repressions and resolved his own human but poorly managed conflicts, he will be able to understand, liberate and heal the patient. It will then be recognised that *locking up the mentally ill is not only inhumane, but also largely unnecessary and without purpose.*

How much easier it will be to gain what we demand first and foremost from the psychiatrist and the nurse, their patience, if the patient's strange behaviour, senseless speech, aimless actions, disorder and agitation are all considered to have meaning. Everything we cannot explain in any way with our logic makes us impatient, causes annoyance or provokes laughter. Psychoanalysis reveals the meaning of these emotions to us and makes it possible to react to the patient's behaviour not with suppressed anger, but with understanding.

A doctor at the Yellow House who has not undergone the process of correcting his own psyche, that is, gone through analysis, may be a good, self-sacrificing and patient person, but he will never be able to understand his patients.

And until he understands that the patient's words do make sense, or is at least no longer convinced that they do not, the patient will not be granted deliverance by even the most sensitive doctor. Even in the doctor's eyes, the patient is insane.

What to do with the Patient?

Cure him!

What do we do today? Call ambulances and police.

I know, my friend! I know! Exaggeration. Perhaps this isn't the best way to commit it to parchment, but it is how I see the situation. And it is true that patients in many institutions are treated differently. And great progress has been made in terms of physical treatment to cure even the most severely mentally ill. But this is not what we're talking about. It does not change what must remain constant in addition to all this: the perception we are fed of the being and meaning of the mental patient.

They speak of the mentally ill and think of the lunatic.

There is no such thing as a lunatic!

There are as many types of patient as there are of people. Everyone needs different treatment and care. But the situation is whatever was pronounced by the magistrate who brought the patient up in a straitjacket:

"If there is fire, we march out with the fire hose, and if the medical officer declares someone mentally ill, we march out with the straitjacket."

To them, the madman is mad, and they fail to see the hidden meaning in him.

There is no such thing as 'the mentally ill'. There are people. It is the height of ignorance and shamefulness to treat them all the same, as lunatics, to lock them up just the same, to place them under guardianship, and to exercise unbridled control over them.

How many times I have awkwardly sensed the many gross indiscretions committed by the tender family around the patient, like fussing over him in whispers while he imperceptibly observes his environment, which completely misunderstands him, and assesses how it is that they, without asking his permission and against his will, seem to be presiding over him.

The Madhouse – A Family Home[71]

In a locked house!

Locking up the patient does little to cure him. If a doctor or nurse does not do everything in his or her power to gradually free the patient from the locked building, the patient will sink deeper and deeper into it. Or he will do what some other patients do: recover in spite of the Yellow House.

Shame and humiliation often extinguish the last spark of self-esteem and hope in patients who end up in the Yellow House.

Dear friend, proclaim to the world:

"The Yellow House must be wiped from the face of the earth!"

But what should take its place?

Something where the structure of the bars, how the walls are painted and the features of the floors, beds, bathrooms, windows and doors, all matters of such important concern today, cease to be issues. The point is that the place in which the patient resides should not be a barracks, a monastery, a hospital, or even a sanatorium, *but simply a home!*

Let there be a hearth, with an understanding family!

As long as our culture is founded on the family, the family is the only place for those made sick by culture to heal!

Every patient, including those with physical conditions, in essence becomes a child. He seeks help, a mother.

The best nurse, and also sometimes the best doctor, is actually the mother. I know, not always. In fact, sometimes not at all. But wherever the patient goes, he or she is searching for a home and a mother. A mother, even when she is in conflict with her own mother, or even more so.

Every patient is a Cadavi.

The Yellow House is as inhospitable as a besieged military fortress.

There is nothing of the home in it, of the intimacy of the nest! The mother is missing from it!

There are patients for whom it would be cruel malpractice to drag them out of their families. Just as there are also cases when patients should not be left with their families. These patients need to be placed in another family. This family will provide familial care, even if it is unaware that what it is doing represents, as a significant advance in therapy, a unique method of psychological healing for the mentally ill.

The time will come when, in the hands of the doctor, the family will be *the instrument of healing, one woven from psychological strands.*

•

A person cut off from life and locked up in the Yellow House is constantly touched and scoured by existence, no matter how many stone walls and bars he is confined behind. Life still washes him, like the sea does a coral island, shaping him, enlarging him and wearing away at him... Life: the family members of the doctors and nurses, as well as the birds in the gardens, visitors seeing other patients, children, inspectors, curious ladies, students, the chimney sweep, the electrician... they all comprise parts of life, and they all weave something into the patient's dream world... Life comes and comes, my friend, *for life is too strong for our locks and keys.*

Life doesn't come along without purpose, it wants something... the sad thing is that we doctors don't yet know what it is. *How to use the healing power of life to the benefit of the patient fleeing from it.*

You can have no idea of the wonderful change that once took place in the restless women's ward when the sound of an infant's crying was suddenly heard from behind a cell door. A woman had given birth. At dawn, the patients woke one another:

"Get up, quickly, a baby has been born!"

With flushed faces and bright eyes, they crowded around the cell door. They laughed softly, holding back their breath. They motioned each other to be silent. They arrived on tiptoes, some of them patients who hadn't risen from their beds in years. Suddenly, they became humans and mothers, they watched the baby cry in the dawn light. Some stood there with tears in their eyes. They became living, actual human beings... For an hour, a day, a few days, they were healed... The sound of the child had teased them up to life's surface.

The infant had redeemed them.

For a few days, while the infant was there among the patients, the ward was transformed... Everyone had something worth living for. In reality, it was barely anything – because it was hardly possible for one or the other of them to take the little one in her arms and coo at it – and yet it meant so much. After that, the 'child of the ward' had to be taken away, and everything returned to how it used to be.

We must be both scientists and poets to understand what life wants from us. We see the same thing. The patient seizes something from everyone and creates stories and relationships... an imaginary family.

It is a matter of certainty that it is in the family situation that the patient must repeat and then properly resolve the childhood conflict – also in the family – from which he or she emerged with a fateful injury.

•

The treatment of patients instinctively developed in the direction of family care.

Records state that the mentally ill of Belgium, seeking a cure for their afflictions, would make a pilgrimage to the town of Geel, site of the grave of a mentally ill 6th-century princess who fled from her own father's amorous pursuits to her death.[72] There is deep significance in the fact that the mentally ill intuitively sought a cure from this Saint Dymphna, martyr of the Oedipus conflict. The local population took some of these mentally ill pilgrims under their care, and thus family care of mental patients gradually developed in the town. When I visited, there were more than two thousand mentally ill people living in the small town. In addition to the two thousand unconfined patients, there were one hundred others – alternating – in the closed infirmary.

Instead of today's mass accommodation, small nursing homes will be built, including for patients who require confinement, as has already been attempted in some places. There, the patient enters a free life, but within the boundaries of a medically supervised and understanding family. Eventually, the individual will return to his or her own family.

In the meantime, the patients themselves also carry out the work of enlightening and liberating the healthy.

Healthy people will no longer need to see patients as lunatics.

The healthy must be healed!

The Many Yellow Houses

Our culture is increasingly overrun by neurosis!

Why? Perhaps there are too many prohibitions. Taboos.

I, my friend, view all these prohibitions as a multitude of small compartments in which instinctive desires have been locked. Each prohibition is a little yellow house unto itself. Then, all of a sudden, there are a great number of little yellow houses, and all those locked-in desires break out. That's why people built the big Yellow House. The Yellow House is itself a symptom in which the repressed, the forbidden returns. When Cadavi fled his mother... the place he fled to was once again the mother.

Humanity has locked itself into compartments, but wherever it ends up, it is again behind bars. However, this is also the most unbridled kind of freedom, the living out of the forbidden desire in fantasy: mental illness and the Yellow House.

This is how the little yellow houses are bound up with the Yellow House.

Once there are no more yellow houses, taboos, within the city, then perhaps there will be no need for a Yellow House outside the city walls.

•

Our culture is increasingly overrun by neurosis!

The legion of neurotics:

Those who fear going out in the street or being in a closed room, or fear noise, silence, animals, disease, a sudden death or a slow one, impoverishment, being buried alive, going insane and above all – when love calls: impotence...

Those who are held back by fear in their work, leisure, joy and sorrow. Those who feel themselves to blame and must compulsively count their steps, who write down their words in order to prove an alibi against unthinkable accusations, who are tormented at night by an incomprehensible sense of guilt and, above all, those who – when love calls – dare not love...

Those full of grand plans but who, plagued by feelings of wretchedness, are unable to take a single step in life, and despise love...

Those who hate the ones they love, are engaged in constant battles with their parents, who torment themselves and their spouses with jealousy, and, above all, those who force suffering and pain onto the moment of erotic pleasure...

And the legion of suffering children: those whose souls are torn in two because the Ego-ideals of their parents were torn in two. Those who fear, dissemble and hate, and those who feign love...

Not one of them is mentally ill: they are healthy and neurotic, but their willpower is gone... They are those who build up their strength every morning with calming sentiments, only to have it crushed by the day, the weather, a piece of news, an encounter, a word, a gesture.

They are those tossed around by anger with nowhere to go!

A legion of neurotics whose suffering is exacerbated by the fact that no one wants to try to understand them. They are those who are not seen as ill, but as weak-willed, for which they are mocked. They are the ones who envy those afflicted with respiratory disorders, for others consider them to be ill and understand their suffering, and are gentle and patient with them...

They are those to whom even the doctor sometimes recommends nothing more than to banish all that nonsense from their heads!

"You just need to want it!"

As if it was not life, education, and all the prohibitions that blocked off the will at its source.

Understanding, sympathy and help for the neurotic are nowhere to be found!

When you have taken the reader this far, my friend, tell him that there is indeed understanding, point out that there is sympathy and call out to him:

"Help is at hand!"

There is a cure! There are many more neurotics and psychotics than doctors know about. Many are ill in secret and are cured in secret. The great catharsis of life, acts of rebellion and falling asleep have in themselves more than once served as the cure.

But the neurotic will search for the same means of escape as that sought by a trapped fly attempting to pass through a glass wall... Strength, energy and will are all he needs to take on that impossible wall! *When, in fact, it is those trapdoors that should be opened first behind which the prohibitions have locked away the will.*

There is a logical escape route: the same as that which the patient entered the trap through.

The path to healing can lead through the past, through the terrifying and disquieting fog.

This is the difficult path of psychoanalysis.

Within Each of Us is the Primal Animal, the Secret to Our Misery and Happiness

It is true that neurosis yields cultural fruits of infinite value. Artistic, poetic works and humanitarian acts for the public good.

Art is a vast expression of humanity's primal longing for the past. But the artist, the poet, does not wish to break away from reality for good, but from the past, to which he ran with a painful and playful desire before returning to the present. Art is not a tragic expression of humanity's longing for the past, like mental illness, but rather a triumphant hymn... When millions of people immerse themselves in the Bible, the writings of Homer, Dante... And when millions sit in darkened auditoriums and listen with bated breath to the miracle, the stream of joy, pouring from Beethoven's symphony, or watch the mysterious story commencing with thick black lines of sound that slowly begin to vibrate before forming into the Rhine quivering in the breaking dawn, and then the resurrected world of the demigods, and then the awful buried past we all share and long for...

•

In the souls of poets, heroes and lunatics, the human order struggles with an unknown, terrifying realm of instinct.

One day, perhaps, people will be able to reconcile the harmony of love and hate, and life and death, with the demands of culture. When, instead of inordinate suppression of instincts, the healthy interest of the individual and the legitimate demands of the culture merge into an optimal harmony...

Neither wild animals nor human populations could ever be completely subjugated by a conqueror in such a way that he completely deprived them of their will and the possibility of life. Man domesticated wild animals and gave culture to primitive peoples. History proves that those oppressed by force either rebel or perish.

And, my friend, tell the people this:

"We must live with our primal wild animals! If they perish, we perish along with them."

Farewell

The autumn rain slowly drums on the streets...

Will people come, full of anxiety about what will happen if our instincts are released? I don't know if it is always possible or necessary to calm the fearful.

In any case, I think it is no longer up to us to release the instincts. The war has subsided, but it did not heal the people... The two enormous camps huffing and puffing at each other have reconciled, but arising in their place are a thousand minor wars. They call them racial, religious, national and class struggles, and they do not even suspect these ideologies to be merely the worn-out uniforms of ailing soldiers. However, what drives the marching soldiers into battle with the whip of love turned to hate is none other than the eternal rulers, even in their exile, of the living:

Primary drives!

Indeed, the real reason for their struggle is to merge the troubled instincts into a new harmony.

However, those wishing to heal a humanity feverish with hatred and sickness are either lying to it, denying the existence of such instincts, or, if they admit that these drives do in fact exist, they attempt to stifle them through force. My friend, it is the same old song again:

Lies or violence.

Remember: the ill are taken to the Yellow House by force or by cunning.

They hardly stop to think there might be a third way, the easiest way:

The truth!

"You have primary drives that you are

ashamed of. It is because of them that you have fallen ill. Become familiar with them and you will be cured through them. Instead of being shocked and afraid, look at what lurks in the depths of the emotions that threaten your morals."

Not long ago, a civil-minded society championing sexual ethics and hygiene came out strongly against the cult of nudism, justifying its stance with the argument that losing one's modesty is the first sign of mental illness. So let's all be modest!

It is true that some sufferers of mental illness cast off their clothes and use obscene language: there are even young girls, chaste women, who have never uttered a suggestive word in their lives, but who, upon the onset of their illness, start to talk obscenely, tear off their clothes and display their genitalia. How much they misunderstand this symptom, those who draw from it the simple conclusion: "But be modest, people!"

This is the symptom: a revolt against sexual morality that weighed excessively on the instincts. The illness: a rebellion against clothes, against false veils; an escape from the unbearable burdens of social responsibilities, instructions and prohibitions. Is it truly appropriate to consider making these instructions stricter without considering the power of instinct?!

•

And then there will come people demanding I provide a work plan! My friend, I have no plan, and advice is rarely worth much.

My objective was to work for the liberation of the mentally ill. I wanted to shine a light on the thicket of archaic prejudices and promote the dream of a new world. It turned out that the question of the mentally ill is just one aspect of a great tangle of social issues. However, this aspect appears to be a suitable starting point in the process of unravelling the whole thing.

The scope of this work is too great in scale for one man to undertake alone, or for one man to accomplish.

A plan must develop of its own accord!

Joining in will be men who, like myself, are searching for the Unconscious aspect of the psyche. The science of the Unconscious will lead not only the Telemachs to *new areas of work*, but also the scholars of society, war and peace.

From an understanding of our own unconscious desires will arise never before imagined possibilities for the social order. Psychoanalysis will influence and shape society as its new fermenting agent.

Knowledge of the Unconscious equals power. *With the help of the Unconscious, the new man will first come to know the essence of the struggle that mankind has waged through culture, a struggle that ended in mental illness for the individual and war for the masses. Then he will learn to constrain and eventually overcome it.*

This will be the new path of humanity's purpose.

The bitter path of humanity's self-awareness.

•

I am descending once again.[73]

My work is done. My work is just beginning.

I harbour both doubts and hopes.

The memory of an old image is revived within me. The young Telemach once wrote:

"I stand in the revivifying cool of dawn like a border post, a frail man all alone. I sense the dance of a distant world. What shall I do with these people who have lain down here with some secret purpose?! What shall I do with those who dance beyond the mountains?!"

...A little girl stands in front of the nurses' houses.

"Farewell, dear little girl! Your uncle the doctor is leaving."

"Where to?"

Sparkling in the child's eyes were a thousand questions. And a thousand words of encouragement...

The era must come when people are more honest with their instincts, when the promise of poets, heroes and fools is fulfilled.

And those who fear that unbridled passions

will result in total destruction will be reassured by the mothers who, with ever-gentle and sure hands, guide the overwhelming love of their sons to new and happier cities.

And I gently stroked the rain-spattered head of the little girl – the mother-to-be...

The mentally ill will be liberated only once the healthy are freed from their own tyranny.

István Hollós

My Farewell to the Yellow House

Notes

1 Camille Robcis, *Disalienation: Politics, Philosophy, and Radical Psychiatry in Postwar France* (Chicago: University of Chicago Press, 2021) p.3.

2 The albums of cut-outs (1931-1936) preserved in the Psychiatric Art Collection Archive of the Hungarian Academy of the Sciences contain photos recording the meeting between performers, doctors, and patients.

3 Zsigmond Justh, *Napló* [*Diary*] (Budapest: Athenaeum, 1941) pp.364-366.

4 Sándor Ferenczi, 'Confusion of Tongues between Adults and the Child' [1933], in Sándor Ferenczi, *Final Contributions to the Problems and Methods of Psycho-Analysis*, ed. by Michael Bálint, trans. by Eric Mosbacher (London: Karnac, 1994) pp.156–167.

5 The family name 'Pfeiflein' condenses both maternal and paternal references, suggesting that the author, Doctor Telemach Pfeiflein, and the publisher, István Hollós, are alter-egos. Hollós' mother was called Borbála Pfeiffer, and her first husband was a medical doctor; she then married the father of István Hollós, a tailor called Ignácz Hesslein.

6 See the letter from István Hollós to Paul Federn, 17 February 1946, in *Psyché*, 38th ser., 4 (March 1974) pp.266-268. See also three excerpts from the letter in the preface to the French edition of *My Farewell to the Yellow House*, by Eva Gerő-Brabant, included in this volume.

7 Pál Ignotus. (1993). 'Polányi Mihály Magyarországa', trans. Nyírő Zsuzsa, *Polanyiana*, 3rd ser., 2 (1993) p.91.

8 This deeply-rooted cultural tradition survived political changes, and was still prevalent in the circles of intellectuals in the post-war years, and until the seventies. Examples include the pulmonologist and art collector László Levendel (1920-1994) and the psychologist, therapist, and advocate of democratic psychiatry, the 'bricoleur' intellectual Ferenc Mérei (1909-1986).

9 Emese Lafferton, *Hungarian Psychiatry, Society and Politics in the Long Nineteenth Century* (Cham: Palgrave Macmillan, 2022) p.162.

10 ibid., p.161, p.164.

11 ibid., p.104.

12 ibid., pp.101-146.

13 ibid., pp.165-178.

14 István Zsakó, 'Az elmebetegek családi ápolása mint a faluegészségügy fejlesztési tényezője' ['Family care for the mentally ill as a means of improving village healthcare'], *Népegészségügy* (1929) 18-19. Offprint, Archive of the Psychiatric Art Collection, the Hungarian Academy of Sciences, Budapest.

15 See official notification of the release from service of István Hollós, July 25 1922, with the signature of Gusztáv Oláh, Ferenczi House Archive, Sándor Ferenczi Society, ref. num.: Hol/I/1/17.

16 See letter from Gusztáv Oláh to István Hollós, July 8 1898, Ferenczi House Archive, Sándor Ferenczi Society, ref. num.: Hol/I/1/15.

17 Ferenc Erős, 'Hollós István tanulmánya elé' ['Preface to an essay by István Hollós'] *Pszichológia,* 5 (1985) 612–615.

18 István Hollós, 'A lipótmezei áll. elmegyógyintézet 40 évi betegforgalma' ['Patient turnover at the State Mental Hospital – Lipótmező – over 40 Years], *Orvosi Hetilap,* 53 (1909), *Elme- és Idegkórtan Melléklet,* 75.

19 István Hollós, 'Über Struktur und Dynamik des psychischen Apparates', *Imago,* 17th ser., 4 (1931) 495-517.

20 István Hollós, 'Über das Zeitgefühl', *Internationale Zeitschrift für Psychoanalyse,* 8 (1922) 421-439.

21 The published German-language paper version of the lecture appeared in the

Zeitschrift only in late 1924, when Rank was leaving the camp of psychoanalysis. Through Ferenczi, Hollós must have been well acquainted with the story of the debate, and in a dissociative note, he indicated his difference from Rank's work.

22 István Hollós, 'Über das Zeitgefühl', *Internationale Zeitschrift für Psychoanalyse* 8 (1922) 424.

23 István Hollós and Sándor Ferenczi, *Zur Psychoanalyse der paralytischen Geistesstörung* (Leipzig, Vienna, Zurich: Internationaler Psychoanalytische Verlag, 1922) pp. 3-36.

24 Ferenczi told Freud about the preparation of the book and their collaboration: 'The boardinghouse [where Ferenczi and his wife stayed in that time] is near the insane asylum where Hollós is chief physician of a section. We see each other often and want to do psychiatric work together.' See *The Correspondence of Sigmund Freud and Sándor Ferenczi, Volume 3: 1920-1933*, ed. by Ernst Falzeder and Eva Brabant, trans. by Peter T. Hoffer (London: The Belknap Press, 2000) p.33.

25 Ferenczi, as early as August 15 1920, wrote to Freud with a precise summary of the

subject and purpose of the project: 'You see, I came upon the idea that the organic psychoses, which demonstrate so much similarity to the functional (narcissistic) psychoses, are actually cerebral patho-neuroses, which form their symptoms on a similarly regressive path as the functional ones. The cases speak in favour of the correctness of this assumption. So, almost all psychoses should be considered as belonging to the narcissistic group. If I remember correctly, that also corresponds to your expectations'. See ibid., and also Sándor Ferenczi, *Thalassa. A Theory of Genitality* [1924], trans. by H. A. Bunker (London, New York: Karnac, 1989).

26 See András Lengyel, 'Kosztolányi, Hollós István és a nyelv pszichoanalitikus fölfogása' ['Kosztolányi, István Hollós and a Psychoanalytic Approach to the Language'], *Új Forrás*, 8 (1998) 52–65.

27 This is articulated in a German text, Der Aufstieg von der Triebsprache zur menschlichen Sprache. This remained fragmentary, but fortunately the manuscript was preserved by Iván Fónagy, who passed it to Ferenc Erős. It is now held in the Ferenczi House Archive. Published in Hungarian, together with the scientific introduction

by Iván Fónagy. See: 'Az ismeretlen Hollós István' ['The Unknown István Hollós'] *Thalassa*, 13th ser., 1-2 (2002) pp 74–117.

28 Handwritten workbook. Manuscript kept by the Ferenczi House Archive, Sándor Ferenczi Society, ref. num.: Hol/I/1/19. See also the mention of József, as a patient in the care of Hollós, in Eva Gerő-Brabant's 'Preface' below.

29 István Hollós, Beszélgetés az alkoholizmusról [Dialogue on Alcoholism] [1908], *Egészség-Naptár*. (A copy is kept in the Ferenczi House Archive, Sándor Ferenczi Society, ref. num.: Hol/I/2/1).

30 Ferenczi House Archive, Sándor Ferenczi Society, ref. num.: Hol/III/2/57.

31 This translation was made possible via a UKRI Frontier Research Grant (ERC grant guarantee), awarded by the Engineering and Physical Sciences Research Council [grant number EP/X022064/1], for the project titled: 'FREEPSY: Free Clinics and a Psychoanalysis for the People: Progressive Histories, Collective Practices, Implications for our Times' (PI: Raluca Soreanu). The German edition is: István Hollós, *Hinter der gelben Mauer: Von der Befreiung*

des Irren (Stuttgart–Leipzig–Zürich: Hippokrates-Verlag, 1928); the French: István Hollós, *Mes Adieux a la Maison Jaune*, trans. by Judith Dupont (Paris: Éditions du Coq-Héron, 1986); and the Italian: István Hollós, *I miei addii alla Casa Gialla*, trans. by M. Alessandrini (Rome: Edizioni Scientifiche Ma.Gi, 2000).

32 After the closing of Lipótmező in 2008, the collection was transported to the Hungarian Academy of Sciences. Now it resides in the Institute of Art History (HUN REN Research Centre for the Humanities) as the Psychiatric Art Collection of the Hungarian Academy of the Sciences.

33 Sándor Ferenczi, *The Clinical Diary of Sándor Ferenczi* [1932], ed. by Judith Dupont, trans. by Michel Bálint, and N. Z. Jackson (Cambridge, Mass.: Harvard University Press, 1995).

34 Sigmund Freud, 'Letter from Sigmund Freud to C. G. Jung, January 17, 1909', in *The Freud/Jung Letters: The Correspondence Between Sigmund Freud and C. G. Jung*, ed. by William McGuire, trans. by Ralph Mannheim and R. F. C. Hull (Princeton: Princeton University Press, 1974) pp.196-197.

35 See François Roustang, *Un destin si funeste* (Paris: Minuit, 1978); specifically the chapter analysing the relationship between Freud and Jung: 'Chacun sa folie' ('Each his own madness').

36 Sigmund Freud, 'Letter from Sigmund Freud to C. G. Jung, February 17, 1908' in *The Freud/Jung Letters*, pp.120-121.

37 Sigmund Freud, 'Letter from Freud to Lou Andreas-Salomé, August 1, 1919' in *Sigmund Freud and Lou Andreas-Salomé: Letters*, ed. by Ernst Pfeiffer, trans. by William and Elaine Robson-Scott (New York: W. W. Norton, 1985) pp.98.

38 István Hollós, 'About a patient who recited poetry' [1914], *Nyugat*, 8th ser., 5 (March 1914) 333-340 [in Hungarian, cited in the French edition of this book].

39 ibid.

40 cf. Eva Brabant, 'Le coupable innocent: Le poète Attila Josse et ses psychanalyses - Histoire de la réaction thérapeutique négative', *Coq-Héron*, 84 (1982).

41 See *Psyché*, 38th ser., 4 (March 1974), pp.266-268. Ernst Federn (Vienna) brought to our

attention this extract from a letter to Paul Federn from the Hungarian psychoanalyst I. Hollós, one of the pioneers of the psychoanalytic exploration of the psychoses. In this letter, Hollós talks about how he and his wife narrowly escaped being murdered when they had been practically condemned to be shot by the Hungarian fascists (Arrow Crosses). [Note of the journal *Psyché*.]

42 The Swedish ambassador provided Swedish passports for Jewish citizens in order to help them escape to the United States.

43 This was the cellar of the police barracks where political prisoners were held.

44 Sándor Ferenczi, 'Notes and Fragments' [1930–32], *International Journal of Psychoanalysis*, 30 (1949) p.237.

45 'Elmebeteg' in Hungarian. This word is no longer used by professionals today.

46 'Tébolyda' is an old-fashioned term, corresponding to 'lunatic asylum'.

47 A historical region in the southeast of Hungary demarcated by the Maros-Tisza river and by the Hungarian-Romanian border (after 1920). The historical image of the

multi-ethnic population inhabiting this territory is that of a very independent, even rebellious one. Storm Corner is also the title of a sociological novel by Géza Féja, contemporary to Hollós, focusing on the theme of rebelliousness.

48 This is a tongue-twister in German, meaning 'third mounted mountain artillery brigade'. The writing here appears agglutinated. It would be correctly written 'dritte berittene Gebirgsartilleriebrigade'.

49 'Dementia praecox': the old term for 'schizophrenia'.

50 'Attilas': very elegant overcoats.

51 'Kreuzers': small-value copper coins.

52 This is German in the source text. German was commonly spoken in Budapest at the time. In translation it reads: 'Yes, this is the carriage of Emperor Maximilian... That there is poor Rudolf in his crypt...' Kaiser Maximilian, a member of the Habsburg family, was the emperor of Mexico and he was executed by the republican uprising in 1867. Rudolf, the crown prince of the Monarchy committed suicide in 1889.

53 In the original, half in German, half in Hungarian.: 'Ach, der bolond!'.

54 *Die Gartenlaube – Illustrirtes Familienblatt* ('*The Garden Arbor – Illustrated Family Journal*') was an educational and entertaining weekly, the first successful mass-circulation German magazine, published between 1853 and 1944, popular in the Austro-Hungarian Monarchy.

55 Baron Alexander von Bach (German: Alexander Freiherr von Bach) (1813–1893) was an Austrian politician. He is best remembered for instituting a system of centralized control at the beginning of the reign of Emperor Franz Joseph I of Austria.

56 'Hand over your weapon!' In German in the original.

57 'Ihre Majestät': 'Her Majesty'. In German in the original.

58 'Betegek betegei' is a play on words in Hungarian. 'Beteg' means both 'sick person' and 'patient'. The meaning is that sick people have their own sick.

59 In Sanskrit, 'That art thou'. It is one of the 'The Mahāvākyas', or 'The Great Sayings'

of the Upanishads, as characterized by the Advaita school of Vedanta.

60 In Hungarian, the title of Dániel Berzsenyi's (1776–1836) poem is 'Osztályrészem'.

61 Translation made by the translator.

62 Translation made by the translator.

63 'State unchanged'.

64 'It will always return'. In French in the original.

65 Hollós uses the verb 'Amerikázni', 'to American', meaning to engage in slowdown or go-slow industrial action – a strike where workers do not completely put down their tools, but work less.

66 Philippe Pinel (1745–1826) was a French physician who pioneered the humane treatment of the mentally ill. In 1792 he became the chief physician at the Paris asylum for men, Bicêtre, and made his first bold reform by unchaining patients. He did the same for the female patients of Salpêtrière when he became the director there in 1794.

67 Clifford Whittingham Beers (1876–1943) was an American author and influential figure in the field of mental hygiene in the United States. Beers suffered severe episodes of depression and anxiety. He was abused during his confinement at various private and state mental institutions. He shared his struggles with mental illness openly in his autobiography, *A Mind That Found Itself* (1908). The book served as a call to reform mental health care.

68 Translation made by the translator, of the final verse of poem 'Feltámadott a tenger', or 'The Whole Sea Has Revolted'.

69 Hollós here quotes from Sigmund Freud's 1917 paper 'A Difficulty in the Path of Psychoanalysis'.

70 In Hungarian, 'lélek'. In a direct translation, 'lélek' means 'soul'. In Hungarian, psychoanalysis is termed 'lelekelemzes', which literally means 'soulanalysis'. Here, the meaning is thus closer to 'psyche'.

71 The institution of 'family care', launched in 1905 in Dicsőszentmárton/Târnăveni (situated in Transylvania, next to Nagyszeben/Sibiu) was centred on placing incurable patients in village households, or newly

built colonies close to asylums, or bigger hospital wards, where the host families received income in return.

72 This refers to the pilgrimage to honour Dymphna, a Christian saint in Catholic and Eastern Orthodox traditions, who was martyred by her father, and is believed to have the power to cure mental disorders. As the church of Geel, built in Dymphna's honour, could no longer host the large influx of pilgrims coming to Geel, the townspeople started taking them into their own homes, which began a tradition for the ongoing care of those with psychological conditions that has endured for over 500 years. The patients are called 'boarders' and they are regarded as ordinary and useful members of the town and members of the host family. At its peak in the 1930s, the inhabitants of Geel hosted over 4,000 'boarders'.

73 The Yellow House is on a hill; this will probably have been known to Hungarian readers.

www.ingramcontent.com/pod-product-compliance
Ingram Content Group UK Ltd.
Pitfield, Milton Keynes, MK11 3LW, UK
UKHW041143300926
15471UKWH00012B/119

9 781919 601953